An Education Research Primer

An Education Research Primer

How to Understand,

Evaluate, and Use It

Patricia A. Lauer

JOSSEY-BASS
A Wiley Imprint
www.josseybass.com

Published by Jossey-Bass
A Wiley Imprint
989 Market Street, San Francisco, CA 94103-1741   www.josseybass.com

Readers should be aware that Internet Web sites offered as citations and/or sources for further information may have changed or disappeared between the time this was written and when it is read.

Jossey-Bass books and products are available through most bookstores. To contact Jossey-Bass directly call our Customer Care Department within the U.S. at 800-956-7739, outside the U.S. at 317-572-3986, or fax 317-572-4002.

Jossey-Bass also publishes its books in a variety of electronic formats. Some content that appears in print may not be available in electronic books.

Library of Congress Cataloging-in-Publication Data

Lauer, Patricia A.
  An education research primer : how to understand, evaluate, and use it / Patricia A. Lauer.— 1st ed.
     p. cm.
  Includes bibliographical references and index.
  ISBN 10: 0-7879-8323-3 (alk. paper)
  ISBN 13: 978-0-7879-8323-9
  1. Education—Research. 2. Education—Research—Evaluation. I. Title.
  LB1028.L29 2006
  370.7'2—dc22
                            2006000744

Printed in the United States of America

FIRST EDITION

PB Printing   10 9 8 7 6 5 4 3 2 1

The Jossey-Bass Education Series

Contents

Foreword

THE EMPHASIS on "research based" education decisions is stronger than ever. The stress on selecting research-based programs was part of the Comprehensive School Reform legislation of the 1990s; that stress has increased in this century's No Child Left Behind Act and the legislation creating the Institute for Education Sciences.

Curricula and programs that *claim* to have a strong research basis are widely available. The question is, however, whether these claims are to be believed. If a claim is followed by a citation or a study's reprint, is that enough? Counterclaims about the flaws in many studies make clear that the answer is no. Education practitioners and policymakers need a way of deciding how much credence to give to studies that ostensibly demonstrate research support. They also need to evaluate how tight the link is between the study and the associated claim. Judgments about research require understanding of core research concepts and their role in evaluating research.

For those whose formal training in research is absent, weak, or a distant memory, Pat Lauer's book explains core concepts and principles for judging research claims, with illustrations that show how the concepts should be applied. The book explains key terms such as "experimental" and "qualitative" in everyday language. The research community has not reached consensus on precise definitions of all these terms, but some grasp of their meaning is essential to knowing what characteristics to look for and in which kind of study. Lauer gives guidance on how to judge the relevance of a study, as well as its rigor.

Lauer's book fits well with current national discussions of education research. Principles from the National Research Council report, *Scientific Research in Education,* are a centerpiece of her analysis. Like that volume,

Lauer emphasizes the importance of matching research method to research question. Experiments may be well suited for answering some causal questions, for example, but inappropriate for answering questions about national achievement trends.

For policymakers and practitioners trying to sort through competing claims for what research has shown, this volume offers a way to begin looking carefully at research reports. It stresses getting clarity about what question a study tries to answer, judging whether the method is well matched to the question, and considering how the investigators have guarded against threats to validity. Readers of this book will be able to give closer attention to the quality of research, and may increase their demands for rigorous, relevant research.

Robert E. Floden
Michigan State University

Acknowledgments

THIS BOOK is based on an online research primer developed by Mid-continent Research for Education and Learning (McREL) and the Education Commission of the States (ECS). ECS provided the original impetus for the online primer and the Web design, and Michael Allen of ECS served as principal editor. McREL provided the technical expertise through my authorship. Funding for the online primer was provided by the U.S. Department of Education, under McREL's Regional Educational Laboratory contract and through a grant to ECS from the Fund for the Improvement of Education.*

I was able to convert and expand the online primer into the current book through development support from McREL. I wish to thank several persons at McREL for their assistance with this effort. Thanks go to Adrienne Schure for her guidance and support in developing the book, Zoe Barley and Lou Cicchinelli for their helpful suggestions concerning the content, David Frost for his encouragement and legal advice, and Barbara Aiduk for preparing the document.

---

* The content of this publication does nto necessarily reflect the views or policies of the Department of Education nor does mention of trade names, commercial products, or organizations imply endorsement by the U.S. government.

To the memory of William F. Battig,
an exceptional researcher and mentor

Preface

SOCIAL SCIENTISTS have conducted studies related to education issues for at least a century, but it was the No Child Left Behind (NCLB) Act of 2001 that called unprecedented attention to education research. NCLB requires that decisions about whether education practices are effective be based on research.

With the advent of NCLB, "research-based" has become a term frequently used by educators, developers, and publishers. They recognize that research evidence adds value to their practices, programs, and materials, but what does it mean to be "research-based"? How does one determine whether a research study is "good" or "bad"? What information can different types of research provide?

An Education Research Primer is designed to answer these and other questions asked by those in the education field. The book is intended to help teachers, principals, superintendents, and policymakers better understand research methods so they can be more informed consumers of education research. Others who will find the *Primer* useful are students of teacher preparation and education leadership. Finally, for faculty in education and the social sciences, this book is a reference source on basic research principles and can be used as a supplementary text in research courses.

The underlying theme of *An Education Research Primer* is that information from research is more reliable than information from other sources such as stories, personal experiences, opinions, or logical arguments. The reason is that research uses systematic methods to gather empirical information, that is, information on things that can be observed; for example, student test scores or classroom teaching practices. Without access to education research, educators and policymakers can make decisions that are ineffective or even harmful. However, not all research is created equal. Understanding more about research can help educators and policymakers judge the accuracy of information from different types of studies and enable them to evaluate researchers' or developers' claims about scientific support for their points of view or products.

The goals of the chapters that follow are to help readers (1) understand education research, (2) evaluate whether the research is trustworthy, and (3) determine the usefulness of the research in guiding education practices or policies. What makes *An Education Research Primer* different from typical methodology texts is its organization around the basic knowledge that educators and those new to the field of education research need to know. In contrast to many methodology texts, there is more emphasis on understanding research concepts than on terminology. To help readers gain a conceptual understanding of education research, the book provides numerous examples and other explanatory materials throughout.

The first two chapters provide an overview of education research. Chapter One describes its purpose, and Chapter Two explains how scientific criteria are applied in education research. Chapter Three outlines the different types of education research and defines associated terms. Chapter Four compares the two main categories of education research—experimental and descriptive. Chapter Five explains data collection methods and instruments. Chapters Six through Nine discuss how to evaluate education research studies, and Chapter Ten provides suggestions and a tool for assessing the relevance of studies to practice or policy. The appendices are designed to help the reader with practical information, including tips on reading research reports, a glossary of research terms, advice on how to find research studies, and a tutorial on basic statistics. Glossary terms, upon their first use in the chapter, appear in bold.

Chapter 1

The Purpose of Education Research

THE WORD *RESEARCH* is used in many different ways. For example, people talk about "doing research" on which car to buy. They go to the library to "research" a particular topic such as a law or historical event.

In education, when people refer to research they may mean either empirical or nonempirical studies. Examples of nonempirical studies are studies that research the history of a practice, institution, or individual; explore what a thinker or a number of thinkers have said about a specific topic; or use other written sources to compare education practices in one country with those in another. Empirical research seeks information about something that can be observed in the real world or in the laboratory—what effects a certain kind of professional development has on a teacher's ability to teach, what impact socioeconomic factors have on student performance, whether a particular curriculum improves students' performance in mathematics, and so on.

Reasons to Use or Engage in Research

An understanding of research can help educators and policymakers make evidence-based decisions about education, such as school programming and teaching practice. Information from research is more reliable than information from other sources such as stories, personal experiences, opinions, or logical arguments because research is based on systematic gathering of **empirical information**. For example, how should a legislator decide whether state funds should be used to reduce the size of classes in K–12 schools?

A legislator might make this decision based on (1) an anecdote about how a neighbor's child performed better after transferring to a school with smaller class sizes, (2) a perception that the legislator's own performance was better in smaller classes, (3) a school board member's opinion that smaller class sizes are better for student learning, (4) the logical argument that smaller classes are better for student achievement because students can receive more attention in smaller classes, or (5) a research study showing that students in small classes make larger gains on achievement tests than students in large classes.

Without access to information from research about education practices, educators and policymakers are more likely to make decisions that are ineffective or even harmful.

Because not all research is created equal, educators and policymakers can become better consumers of research by understanding research methods and principles. For example, which of the following research studies provides better support for a decision about reducing class size?

A study of student achievement in small classes compared to large classes in one urban school district

A study of student achievement in small classes compared to large classes in ten rural school districts

The context of a research study (for example, urban versus rural) is one factor to consider. Also important, however, is how the study was conducted. More specifically:

- How were students assigned to the small and large classes?
- Did teachers cover the same curriculum in the small and large classes?
- How was student achievement measured?

In answering these questions, it helps to know

- The best ways to assign students to different types of classes in a research study
- The importance of measuring what and how teachers instruct in different types of classrooms
- The most effective ways to measure student outcomes in a research study

Understanding more about research can help educators and policymakers judge the accuracy of information from different studies and evaluate research that researchers or developers of education materials and programs claim as scientific support for their points of view or products. In other words, policymakers and educators can better determine whether there is scientific evidence that an education program, **intervention,** or practice is effective.

At the school and district levels, education research can help administrators make programming decisions. For example, on what basis should a high school principal decide whether to adopt block scheduling so that students attend class in subject areas only a few days a week instead of five days as in the traditional schedule?

A principal might make this decision based on (1) her own experience that attending class everyday helped her stay on top of class assignments, (2) opinions from other principals that block scheduling does not influence student learning, (3) the logical argument that having classes that are longer in duration but occur less frequently will help students achieve because students will need less time for review and changing classes, or (4) a research study showing that students in high schools with block scheduling perform better on achievement tests than students in high schools with traditional scheduling.

A research study will provide the most reliable information in making this decision because research is based on empirical information (that is, test scores of students in schools that have the two types of scheduling). However, as in the class size example, in order to use research on school programming in decision making, principals need to understand the different types of studies and be able to evaluate the accuracy of the results. For example, which of the following is more useful for deciding whether to implement a block schedule?

> A **longitudinal** interview study of administrators, teachers, and students in five high schools that have used block scheduling for two years
>
> A study of student achievement in ten high schools, half of which are using traditional scheduling and the other half are using block scheduling

At first glance, the student achievement study is more appealing because it examines student outcomes and compares the two types of class schedules. However, more information is needed about how this study was conducted. In this example, the most important question to ask is, *Are there differences between the two types of high schools other than class schedule?*

It is possible that the two types of schools differ on a myriad of factors that can influence student achievement, such as student socioeconomic status, teacher experience, school size, and school location. Unless the researcher controlled for the influence of these **extraneous variables,** the results of the study could be erroneous and lead the principal to make a decision that could be harmful and costly for her high school.

The interview study, depending on how it was conducted, might be more useful, particularly if the schools in the study are similar to the principal's high school. The interview study could provide in-depth information about block scheduling from several different viewpoints and give feedback about student outcomes other than achievement, such as student motivation and attitudes toward school.

This example illustrates the importance of understanding the **research question** that a study addresses and evaluating whether the **research design** of the study is appropriate to the question being asked. However, regardless of the question or design, the **research method** must be without errors that can threaten the **validity** of the results. Knowing what errors to look for in education research studies can help administrators find valid studies on which to base programming decisions.

At the classroom level, education research can help teachers make decisions about their instructional practices. Most teachers would like to know which instructional strategies are effective in helping students learn, but on what basis should a teacher judge effectiveness? The instructional strategies that his own teachers used to help him learn? Opinions from other teachers about what works for the students in their classrooms? Or research showing that the use of certain instructional strategies such as cooperative groups can increase student achievement?

It is well known that teachers in the absence of other information tend to adopt instructional practices that their own teachers used. It is also an accepted and encouraged practice for teachers to share their knowledge about instruction. However, the problems with both of these information sources are the lack of evidence about instructional effectiveness for more than one student or more than one classroom of students and the lack of empirical documentation. To address these concerns, teachers can examine research on classroom instruction, much of which has been summarized in books and incorporated into professional development trainings. To evaluate the research on instruction, teachers need a basic background in the concepts of education research because there are many developers who will claim to have research-based staff development materials and programs when in fact the research is flawed. In addition, teachers who understand education research can conduct their own classroom studies and use the results to make changes in their practices, an activity referred to as **action research.** Similar to the legislator and policymaker examples, understanding education research can help teachers use research evidence for making effective education decisions.

Current Issues Driving Education Research

The No Child Left Behind (NCLB) Act of 2001 is a major force driving education research and the need for practitioners and policymakers to become more knowledgeable about the conduct of research. NCLB requires states to ensure that children reach high standards of learning so that all students will be proficient after twelve years. Schools and districts that do not achieve adequate yearly progress (AYP) toward this goal for three or more years are required to implement interventions that research indicates are effective in raising student achievement. For example, low-income students in Title I schools that do not achieve AYP are eligible to receive supplementary education services. The state approves these services based on their evidence of effectiveness from research and evaluation studies. Another example is that NCLB urges districts with low-performing Title I schools to develop improvement plans that are based on education research.

This emphasis on research-based evidence in NCLB is increasing the awareness of educators and policymakers about the need for research on school improvement programs. NCLB is encouraging developers of programs, curriculum, and textbooks to demonstrate that their products are effective in raising student achievement and ultimately can help schools achieve AYP. As a result, developers are unlikely to sell their products to schools and districts without claims that the products are research-based, but claims of a research base are insufficient for establishing that an education product will be effective. How the research was conducted is a critical element in deciding whether such claims can be trusted. It is the responsibility of the "buyer" of these education products—policymakers and educators—to be informed about the differences between good and bad research.

Standards-based reform is another force that is driving education research. NCLB embodies the current emphasis in education on standards and accountability, but the standards movement started much earlier. The 1983 publication of *A Nation at Risk* (National Commission on Excellence in Education, 1983) often is cited as the catalyst for events that culminated in a national call for content standards (National Education Goals Panel, 1991). The first content standards were published for mathematics in 1989 (National Council of Teachers of Mathematics, 1989) followed by other content areas in the 1990s (for example, science, language arts, history, geography, social studies). Supporters of standards claim that standards can improve student achievement, equalize student opportunities, coordinate different parts of the education system, provide accurate information to parents and students about expectations, and indicate to stakeholders the degree of student progress in relation to expectations (Ravitch, 1995). Many educators contend that successful implementation of standards-based education requires systemic reform, which is defined as (1) the establishment of student learning standards, (2) the alignment of policies to standards (for example, policies on testing, accountability, teacher professional development, teacher certification), and (3) the restructuring of governance so schools and districts are responsible for developing instruction that meets the standards (Massell, Kirst, & Hoppe, 1997). Research on the elements of systemic reform is an important source of information for policymakers and educators in their search for changes and innovations that can improve the overall functioning of schools and districts. Such research can provide guidance on not only *what* to do that is effective but *how* to do it. For example, schools should adopt professional development that is backed by research showing that the content of the professional development improves teacher instruction. But also important is research showing the most effective ways to implement professional development, such as through teacher collaboration in a community of learners.

Questions on which education programs or interventions work (the theme of NCLB) and how to make education programs or interventions work (the theme of systemic reform) are separate questions that require different types of research, both of which are subject to standards of rigor. Understanding and using these standards to evaluate research can help educators and policymakers identify studies that are both valid and useful in identifying changes that can improve education outcomes.

Chapter 2
Scientific Criteria in Education Research

IS EDUCATION RESEARCH scientific? Can education research be scientific? According to the 2002 National Research Council (NRC) report *Scientific Research in Education,* science is the same in all fields of study, whether it is chemistry, economics, or education. What determines the scientific quality of a research study is the degree to which the study follows the principles that underlie science. The NRC identified six guiding principles for scientific research. The actual principles are quoted here verbatim from the NRC; the further elaboration of each principle paraphrases NRC's discussion of the principles and includes explanatory text that is original to this primer.

The National Research Council's Guiding Principles for Scientific Research

Scientific Principle 1: Pose significant questions that can be investigated empirically.

Empirical research involves investigation that uses observations to guide conclusions. Research questions that are significant do one or more of the following:

- Fill in the gaps in what we know about a topic
- Seek to identify why something occurs
- Solve a practical problem
- Test a new idea or hypothesis
- Expand on scientific knowledge from prior **theories** and research

Scientific Principle 2: Link research to relevant theory.

Theories vary in scope; the more well-known scientific theories tend to be broad, such as Einstein's theory of relativity. Theories that are smaller in scope, sometimes referred to as conceptual frameworks, guide most research studies, particularly in the social sciences and education. Nonetheless, such theories provide the reason for the research design and interpretation of the findings. For example, the theory behind teacher professional development is that teacher learning influences instruction, which in turn influences student achievement. This theory is relatively small in scope because it applies only to teacher learning, in contrast to a theory such as Piaget's, which applies to child and adolescent development. Theories that are small in scope, however, can provide the rationale for scientific research.

Scientific Principle 3: Use methods that permit direct investigation of the question.

This principle means that the research method should be appropriate to the research question. The appropriateness of one method over another is the subject of debate. This is particularly true in the social sciences, where research studies usually involve human **subjects.** Principle 3, however, does not focus on a particular research method. Rather, it emphasizes that a report on a research study should indicate the following:

- The link between the research question and the method used and why the method is the most appropriate
- A detailed description of the method and **procedure** so that other researchers can repeat the study
- Possible problems or limitations with the research method

As Principle 1 indicates, science involves the measurement of observations. In social science research, this means that human behavior will be observed, measured, and recorded. The method used to measure observations is critical because errors in measurement can influence the results.

For this reason, research studies should report on the **validity** and **reliability** of the measuring instruments that are used.

Scientific Principle 4: Provide a coherent and explicit chain of reasoning.

Conclusions about the results of research are based on inferential reasoning. This means that researchers make logical judgments based on the results of their research and on conclusions from prior research. The logic of their judgments depends on their research questions and the methods they used. An important part of this logical reasoning is to rule out alternate or **rival explanations,** also referred to as **threats to validity.** To counter such threats, researchers need to indicate in their studies how they avoided or controlled for such errors.

Scientific Principle 5: Replicate and generalize across studies.

Replication means that a researcher who uses the same study method in the same situations or contexts as another researcher can make the same observations and obtain the same results. (Alternatively, the same researcher can obtain the same results on two different occasions.) **Generalization** refers to how much the results can be replicated in different contexts and with different **populations.** When the results of a study can be replicated and generalized, the results can be trusted more than results from studies without these characteristics. Usually, many research studies are needed to produce a body of knowledge that provides this information.

Scientific Principle 6: Disclose research to encourage
professional scrutiny and critique.

Through this principle, the National Research Council emphasizes that the accumulation of scientific knowledge depends on its dissemination to members of the scientific community for professional critique. Researchers should submit their reports to journals and publications that require **peer review.** Presentations on research at professional conferences also provide the opportunity for critique. To facilitate scrutiny, researchers should keep accurate and accessible records of their investigations so they can provide information for review purposes. For education research to advance, the community of education researchers must enforce the norms of scientific research when judging education research studies.

Scientifically-based Research

The National Research Council's report did not endorse a specific research method. Instead it argued that scientific research in education is possible with a variety of methods, as long as the method matches the research question being investigated. In contrast, the No Child Left Behind (NCLB) Act of 2001 is very specific about research method. The law makes more than a hundred references to **scientifically-based research** in education. According to NCLB, scientifically-based research is rigorous, systematic, objective, empirical, peer reviewed, and relies on multiple measurements and observations, preferably through experimental or quasi-experimental methods (No Child Left Behind Act of 2001). This definition affects the types of research that service providers can use to justify federal expenditures on education programs. For example, states seeking funds from the Reading First Initiative must contract with an entity that conducts *scientifically-based* reading research. The U.S. Department of Education's Institute of Education Sciences has released a publication that elaborates the concept of scientifically-based research. It is entitled *Identifying and Implementing Education Practices Supported by Rigorous Evidence: A User Friendly Guide* and can be viewed on the Web at http://www.ed.gov/rschstat/research/pubs/rigorousevid/index.html or downloaded at http://www.ed.gov/rschstat/research/pubs/rigorousevid/rigorousevid.pdf.

Scientifically-based research, as defined in NCLB, has been referred to as the "gold standard" for research on the effectiveness of education programs and policies. It is a goal of the U. S. Department of Education (2002) to "transform education into an evidence-based field" (p. 59) by giving funding preference to research and evaluation projects that employ the gold standard. More specifically, new research projects funded by the department that address causal questions should use experimental research designs (also referred to as randomized controlled trials) or **quasi-experimental research designs.**

The following is an example of a causal question: *Does a new mathematics curriculum improve student achievement?* An answer to this question could come from a variety of sources: teachers' opinions expressed in interviews, the curriculum developers' claims that students who used the materials improved their math scores, a principal's experiences with the curriculum as described in an education journal. Although these different sources of knowing can be informative, they do not provide rigorous evidence that the curriculum improves student achievement. Obtaining this type of evidence requires an experimental research design such as in the following example:

> A publisher hires a firm to conduct a research study of a new mathematics curriculum it is considering for publication. Four school districts are recruited to participate. Half the schools in the district are randomly assigned to use the new curriculum while the other half are assigned to continue using the curriculum that is already in place. Results indicate that students using the new curriculum improved their mathematics test scores more than students using the old curriculum. Is this rigorous evidence of the curriculum's effectiveness?

The research design (that is, an experiment) is appropriate to the research question, and so the study has potential to provide rigorous evidence. However, much more information is needed about other aspects of the study. For example, did teachers in the two curriculum groups spend an equal amount of time teaching mathematics? Perhaps teachers using the new curriculum became enthused about doing something differently and devoted more time to teaching mathematics than the other teachers. Also, how many students left the schools during the course of the study? Maybe more students left the schools that were using the new curriculum and the students that stayed were higher achievers than those that left.

The point is that rigorous research involves more than appropriate methods. The research needs to be conducted in ways that rule out alternative explanations for the results. This primer is designed to help educators identify such alternative explanations (also called threats to validity).

It is important to ensure that new education practices have rigorous evidence to back their use for several reasons. In NCLB, the reason is primarily a financial one. What return can taxpayers expect from investing federal money in new programs designed to improve education? It makes sense to not invest in a program that lacks evidence of effectiveness. Another reason concerns educators. More than ever before principals and teachers are being asked to change what they do in schools and classrooms. Change without results wastes the time and energy of the nation's educators. Finally, what about the effects of untested practices and programs on the nation's children? Research suggests that poor teaching can harm students' progress in schools, and the same may be true for other aspects of education, such as curriculum. Children are entitled to an education that is based on evidence of effectiveness in helping them learn.

The What Works Clearinghouse

One of the strategies the U.S. Department of Education is using to transform education into an evidence-based field is the creation of the What Works Clearinghouse (http://www.whatworks.ed.gov/). Established in 2002 by the department's Institute of Education Sciences, the What Works Clearinghouse (WWC) is designed to provide educators, policymakers, and researchers a source of scientific evidence on education **interventions** that "work." The WWC produces study, intervention, and topic reports. Study reports provide information on individual studies of a specific intervention; for example, a particular mathematics curriculum for middle school. Intervention reports summarize the outcomes of all the studies on the intervention that the WWC reviewed. Topic reports compile the results of the reports on different interventions related to the same broad topic (for example, curriculum-based interventions for increasing middle school math achievement) and compare the interventions on the strength of their research methods and findings.

To understand the work of the WWC, it is important to know about the WWC's stringent review process. First there is an extensive search for published and unpublished research studies related to an intervention. Then the studies undergo screening for their relevance to the intervention and the use of appropriate methods and measures. Studies that meet the screen are further reviewed and assigned one of three ratings: (1) "Meets Evidence Standards," (2) "Meets Evidence Standards with Reservations," and (3) "Does Not Meet Evidence Screens." The WWC supports the U.S. Department of Education's gold standard for research, which is that causal questions about interventions (that is, the effects of an intervention on student achievement) should be answered with experimental research designs.

The WWC answers questions about the effectiveness of interventions based on studies that use specific research methods—primarily experimental and quasi-experimental designs. In general, the WWC does not answer questions about how to implement an intervention or about the influences of school and classroom contexts on intervention implementation. As the NRC (2002) report suggests, these types of questions are best answered using nonexperimental methods, which although they do not meet the "gold standard," can nonetheless provide scientific evidence related to inquiries such as, *What is happening? How is something happening? Why is something happening?*

In the next chapter, this primer provides guidance on the different types of research questions and the corresponding types of research methods. Following chapters present criteria for evaluating the scientific rigor or validity of studies that use different methods.

Chapter 3

The Types of Education Research

EDUCATION RESEARCH DIFFERS along several dimensions. These dimensions include (1) the type of question that the research seeks to answer, (2) the research design or particular plan for gathering data, (3) the type of data collected, and (4) the goal of the research. In general, the first two are the most important dimensions for understanding and evaluating research studies.

Descriptive and Experimental Research

There are two basic types of education research: **descriptive research** and **experimental research.** Each type answers different research questions and uses different research designs to collect **data.** Exhibit 3.1 shows the relationships among the type of research, research questions, and research designs.

Descriptive Research Questions and Designs

Descriptive research is used to answer descriptive research questions: *What is happening? How is something happening? Why is something happening?*
Examples are

What is the average number of staff development hours per year for teachers in the United States?

What is the association between student–teacher ratios and student achievement in the state's elementary schools?

How do teachers design standards-based lesson plans?

Why do teacher qualifications influence instruction?

EXHIBIT 3.1

Relationships Among Research Type, Question, and Design

Type of Research

    Descriptive

Research Question

    What is happening?

    How is something happening?

    Why is something happening?

Research Design

    Simple descriptive

    Comparative descriptive

    Correlational

Type of Research

    Experimental

Research Question

    Does something cause an effect?

Research Design

    Experimental

    Quasi-experimental

Descriptive research designs include the following:

- Simple descriptive
- Comparative descriptive
- Correlational

A **simple descriptive** research design is used when data are collected to describe persons, organizations, settings, or phenomena. For example, a researcher administers a survey to a **random sample** of teachers in the state in order to describe the characteristics of the state's **population** of teachers.

With a **comparative descriptive** design, the researcher describes and compares two or more groups of participants (McMillan, 2000). For example, a researcher administers a questionnaire to three groups of teachers about their classroom practices. The teachers are from three schools that vary in terms of how much professional development they provide to teachers. The researcher wants to compare the three groups of teachers to describe the characteristics of the instruction of teachers who are receiving different amounts of professional development.

A **correlational** research design is used to describe the statistical association between two or more variables. For example, a researcher measures the student–teacher ratio in each classroom in a school district and measures the average student achievement on the state assessment in each of these same classrooms. Next the researcher uses statistical techniques to measure whether the student–teacher ratio and student achievement in the school district are connected numerically; for example, when the student–teacher ratio changes in value, so does student achievement. The researcher can then use the student–teacher ratio to predict student achievement, a technique called **regression analysis.** When there is more than one predictor, the technique of **multiple regression analysis** produces a multiple correlation that is used for prediction.

Experimental Research Questions and Designs

Experimental research is used to answer causal research questions: *Does something cause an effect?* For example, does a low student–teacher ratio cause higher student achievement?

Experimental research designs include the following:

- True experimental (also referred to as randomized controlled trials)
- Quasi-experimental

In experimental research, the researcher manipulates or varies an **independent variable** and measures its effects on one or more **dependent variables.** In a **true experimental design,** the researcher **randomly assigns** the participants who are being studied (also called the **subjects**) to two or more **comparison groups.** Sometimes the comparison groups are referred to as **treatment** and **control groups.** Participants in the treatment group receive some type of treatment, such as a special reading program. Participants in the control group do not receive the treatment.

For example, at the beginning of a school year, a researcher randomly assigns all fourth grade classes in a school district to have either a low student–teacher ratio (small class, the treatment group) or a normal student–teacher ratio (large class, the control group). At the end of the school year, the researcher measures each student's achievement via the state assessment and compares the average achievement of students in the two sizes of classes. In this example, class size is the independent variable because class size is being varied or manipulated. Student achievement is the dependent variable because student achievement is being measured. (Note: Researchers conducted a similar experiment in the state of Tennessee starting in 1985. The study is known as Project STAR.)

In a quasi-experimental design, the researcher does not randomly assign participants to comparison groups, usually because random assignment is not feasible. To improve a quasi-experimental design, the researcher can **match** the comparison groups on characteristics that relate to the dependent variable. For example, a researcher selects from a school district ten classes to have low student–teacher ratios and ten classes to maintain their current high student–teacher ratios. The researcher selects the high-ratio classes based on their similarity to the low-ratio classes in terms of student socioeconomic status, a characteristic that is related to student achievement, the dependent variable in the study.

Types of Data: Quantitative and Qualitative

In **quantitative research,** the data are numbers and measurements. In the class-size studies described above, the data are student achievement scores, which generally are numbers (for example, 90 percent) or measurements ("proficient"). In **qualitative research,** the data are **narrative descriptions** and **observations.** For example, a researcher wants to know the characteristics of teachers' instructional practices in small compared to large classes (a comparative descriptive study). The researcher observes the two types of classrooms on several different occasions and documents how teachers are interacting with the students. The researcher also **interviews** teachers about the strategies they use to develop lesson plans. The results from the classroom observations and the interviews are qualitative data. The researcher will report the results through narration such as "most of the teacher–student interactions in large classes concerned discipline issues" and "eight of the teachers interviewed said that they considered class size in developing their lesson plans." Note that it is common to summarize qualitative data by using numbers; for example, "60 percent of the observations of small classes documented the use of cooperative learning groups." However, the data being collected (the implementation of cooperative learning groups) are observations of what is occurring in the classroom, and these observations are being documented, not measured on a numerical scale.

In addition to the type of data collected, there are other important differences between quantitative and qualitative research (Creswell, 2002).

Qualitative research occurs in more natural and less controlled research settings than quantitative research, and qualitative research often uses special methods to collect data, such as **case study** and **ethnography.** These methods reflect the philosophy of qualitative research, which emphasizes in-depth descriptions of persons, behaviors, and contexts. For example, a researcher conducts a case study to learn how a school district adopted standards-based reforms in mathematics and science. The researcher analyzes documents such as policy statements, notes from curriculum meetings, and school improvement plans. The researcher interviews key informants such as district and school administrators, staff developers, math and science curriculum specialists, and a sample of math and science teachers. The researcher observes math and science teacher meetings. Contextual influences such as district demographics and history are documented. All the data are combined and analyzed to produce a case study report of how one district went about adopting standards-based reform.

Distinguishing between the types of data collected (quantitative or qualitative) and the type of research (descriptive or experimental) is often a source of confusion. In general, research studies with experimental, quasi-experimental, or correlational designs collect quantitative data. Research studies with simple descriptive or comparative descriptive designs collect either type of data.

When research collects the two types of data or uses multiple research designs, the approach is called **mixed methods** (Creswell, 2002). For example, a researcher studies standards-based reform by collecting qualitative data from teacher interviews and quantitative data from student achievement scores. The researcher compares the achievement scores of students whose teachers reported in interviews that they were high or low implementers of the standards in their classrooms. This study involves two types of data and also two types of research designs. A simple descriptive design is used to answer the question: What do teachers in a district that has adopted standards-based reform do to implement standards in the classroom? The data used to answer this question are qualitative data from teacher interviews. A comparative descriptive design is used to answer the question: What are the differences in student achievement between teachers who are high versus low implementers of standards? Quantitative data from student tests are used to answer this question.

Currently, some education researchers are hailing the use of mixed methods as a way to provide more complete answers to research questions compared to the use of single-method experimental studies. They view mixed-methods research as a way to supplement "scientifically-based research"—which answers questions about what works—with research that answers questions about how and under what conditions something works. For example, a researcher might study the effects of two reading curricula on student achievement. The researcher uses a true experimental research design and randomly assigns the elementary teachers in a school district to use either curriculum A or curriculum B in their classrooms for the school year. The researcher finds that students in the A classrooms improved their reading more than students in the B classrooms. If the study stops here, the results indicate that one curriculum is better than the other but they do not indicate why or how these results occurred. Perhaps curriculum B provides more teacher guidance and staff development than curriculum A. Interviews of the teachers could shed light on why curriculum A was superior and how to best teach the curriculum. This is important information for both the developers of curriculum A and the schools and teachers who adopt curriculum A on the basis of the research study.

Action Research

Action research differs from other types of education research in its goals and features:

- Collection of data about a current education practice or program and the resulting outcomes
- Reflection on the information acquired
- Development and implementation of an improvement plan (the action)
- Collection of data on the practice or program after changes have been made
- Development of conclusions about the results of the improvement plan

Action research can be conducted by individuals, such as teachers, or by groups of individuals, such as school staffs. The latter is referred to as collaborative action research (Calhoun, 1994).

The following is an example of individual action research:

> A teacher wants to know whether group activities will improve the performance of her students in math. She measures the performance of her students on math problems after using whole-group instruction for three weeks. She then supplements her instruction with small-group learning activities for three weeks and again measures student performance. She finds that student achievement increased with the use of small group activities compared to whole-group instruction. On the basis of these action research results, she changes her approach to teaching math.

And here is an example of collaborative action research:

> The teachers and principal of an elementary school want to improve their students' writing skills. Together they examine student writing samples and identify the specific areas that need improvement. They then purchase a new writing curriculum that teachers implement for eight weeks. During the eight weeks, the teachers and principals meet weekly as a group to discuss progress and problems. At the end of the eight weeks, they compare student writing samples to those obtained prior to implementation of the new curriculum. Because there are improvements in student writing, the school decides to adopt the curriculum on a permanent basis. The teachers and principal agree to continue monitoring the implementation and results of the new writing curriculum.

For practitioners, action research can have several benefits. These include reflection on education practice, identification of strategies for improvement, and acquisition of research skills. Collaborative action research has the additional benefit of engaging teachers and principals in joint work to improve education outcomes.

However, action research has some limitations. Most action research studies use descriptive research designs but attempt to draw conclusions about the effects of an action on some outcome. Action research studies rarely employ experimental methods, such as the use of a comparison group, so conclusions about cause and effect are not reliable in many action research studies. Another limitation is that action research usually is restricted to one classroom or school, so the results often cannot be generalized to other classrooms or schools.

Program Evaluation

Evaluation studies have much in common with research studies, particularly in methods and interpretation. That is, they both use the designs in Exhibit 3.1 and they follow the same guidelines in interpreting results. The primary distinction between the two types of inquiry is their purpose. As Weiss (1998) points out, compared to research, evaluations are more driven by program-derived questions and expected utility. Evaluations are conducted for clients such as school districts or textbook publishers and the client's need for information is central to the design of the evaluation and the reporting of results. This characteristic of evaluations is obvious in the typical evaluation report, which usually includes recommendations to the client on how to improve the program implementation or outcomes.

Evaluations often are labeled according to their general purposes, of which the two primary ones are formative and summative. The purpose of a formative evaluation is to provide information about improving program implementation; that of a summative evaluation is to assess program outcomes and effectiveness. Some evaluations include both formative and summative information.

The following example illustrates how utility and client needs drive evaluation studies:

> A developer hires an evaluator to determine whether a new online professional development program helps elementary teachers improve reading instruction. The developer wants to know whether the delivery of the online sessions for teachers is going smoothly (formative evaluation) and also whether the program causes the teachers to change their instruction (summative evaluation). The evaluator designs a study in which half the elementary schools in the district are randomly assigned to participate in the online program and the other half do not participate. About midway through the program, the evaluator interviews participating teachers about their experiences with the online sessions; for example, whether there were technical difficulties, whether they were able to ask questions as needed. The evaluator writes an interim evaluation report on whether the online program has been implemented as intended and makes recommendations for changes (for example, use a different software or a different discussion format). The interim evaluation report provides formative information to the developer, which helps form the characteristics of the online program. At the beginning and end of the program, the evaluator **surveys** both the participating and nonparticipating teachers and observes their reading instruction. The data from the surveys and observations are analyzed and reported in a final summative evaluation report, which sums up the degree to which the online program achieved its objective of changing teachers' reading instruction.

Chapter 4

Understanding Experimental and Descriptive Research

UNDERSTANDING THE DIFFERENCE between **experimental** and **descriptive** research is a prerequisite for evaluating and using education research. Chapter Three describes the different dimensions along which research can vary, but the most basic dimension is whether a study is descriptive or experimental. (Some sources refer to experimental research as "causal" research and to descriptive as "nonexperimental" research.) This chapter describes the differences and similarities between the two types of research in the questions addressed, the programs investigated, how participants are selected, the types of data collected, and the types of findings. The study examples presented in the main sections are prototypes of actual studies, and they address the common theme of teacher professional development. This is to show that the same topic can be studied by using different types of research, but the conclusions will depend on the research method employed. At the end of the chapter, examples of real studies on other education topics are described.

Experimental Studies

Research Questions

The first step in deciding whether a study is experimental or descriptive is to identify the **research question** that the study is attempting to answer. Experimental research is designed to answer causal questions such as, *Does something cause an effect?* or, *Is this program effective?* The following examples illustrate how causal research questions might be stated in a research report. Note that in many reports the word *cause* is not explicit. If the statement or question implies, however, that an effect (for instance, higher student achievement) will result from something that is varied (say, the effect of more versus less teacher professional development), then the research question is a causal question. Also note, again, that questions are sometimes given in the form of statements:

We hypothesized that increasing the amount of professional development teachers received would increase student achievement.

This study evaluated whether teacher professional development in language arts increases student achievement more than teacher professional development in general teaching strategies.

Does providing teachers with professional development in teaching reading cause their students to have higher achievement in reading?

Treatments

Most education research studies concern a particular education **treatment** or **intervention** designed to improve practices or conditions. Examples of treatments are a reading program, a type of teacher preparation, or a mathematics curriculum. In experimental research, the treatment is called the **independent variable** and refers to what the researcher varies or manipulates to determine whether it has an effect. The following list repeats the research questions listed in the previous paragraph but also highlights the independent variables for those questions:

We hypothesized that increasing the amount of professional development teachers received would increase student achievement *(the amount of professional development)*.

This study evaluated whether teacher professional development in language arts increases student achievement more than teacher professional development in general teaching strategies *(the content of the professional development)*.

Does providing teachers with professional development in teaching reading cause their students to have higher achievement in reading *(the opportunity for professional development)*?

The treatments or programs that are studied in experiments are similar to those studied through descriptive research. For example, teacher professional development can be studied through both types of research, but only experiments systematically vary the professional development and then investigate the effects of these variations. Sometimes the **comparison groups** in experimental research are referred to as **treatment** and **control groups.** Participants in the treatment group receive some type of treatment, such as a special reading program. Participants in the control group do not receive the treatment.

Participants

In both experimental and descriptive research, participants are selected because they possess certain characteristics of interest, such as elementary teacher, third grade student, rural school district. It is the assignment of participants to different study conditions that distinguishes experimental from descriptive research. There are two basic types of experimental **research designs.** In a **true experimental design** (also called a randomized controlled trial), the researcher **randomly assigns** the participants to the different comparison groups. This means that the researcher uses chance procedures to assign participants so that each has the same probability of being selected to a group. Examples of chance procedures are drawing names out of a hat, tossing dice, using a table with random numbers, or using a computer program to generate random numbers.

The following is an example of a true experiment with random assignment:

> A researcher is studying whether teacher professional development increases student achievement. Prior to the beginning of the school year, half the fourth grade teachers in a school district are randomly assigned to receive professional development in reading (the treatment group), and the other half are randomly assigned to receive no professional development in reading (the control group). To conduct the random assignment, each person on the list of fourth grade teachers in the district is assigned a number via a random number generator. Teachers with even numbers are assigned to the experimental group and those with odd numbers are assigned to the control group. At the end of the school year, the achievement gains in reading by the students of the two groups of teachers are compared. It is assumed that because teachers were randomly assigned to the two groups, teacher characteristics that might influence reading achievement favor neither the treatment group nor the control group.

In a **quasi-experiment,** the assignment of participants to comparison groups is not random usually because random assignment is not feasible. Instead, the researcher finds a group of persons who are not receiving the treatment and uses that group as the comparison or control group. In quasi-experiments, researchers often try to match the comparison groups on characteristics that might influence the effects of the treatment. The following is an example of a quasi-experiment with **matching:**

> A researcher is studying whether teacher professional development increases student achievement. The researcher assigns

teachers in an elementary school to the treatment group. For the control group, the researcher finds a school with characteristics similar to those of the treatment school. To conduct the matching, the researcher examines student test scores, the percentage of students with free or reduced lunch, and teacher qualifications and identifies the school that is similar on these characteristics to the treatment school. At the end of the school year, the achievement gains in reading by the students of the two groups of teachers are compared. It is assumed that because the two groups are similar, characteristics that might influence reading achievement favor neither group. However, because matching does not use a chance procedure to assign participants to comparison groups, this assumption might not be true, and for this reason quasi-experiments are considered less rigorous than true experiments.

Data

The **dependent variable** in an experimental research study is the variable that is influenced by the independent variable. In the preceding examples, student achievement is the dependent variable and it is influenced by the independent variable of professional development. The researcher assumes that student achievement *depends* on whether teachers receive professional development. In order to examine this assumption, the dependent variable needs to be measured.

Researchers usually collect **quantitative data** to measure the dependent variables in experimental research. With the emphasis in NCLB on improving student achievement, student scores on achievement tests are the data favored by many experimental researchers. However, experimental studies also investigate other sources of quantitative data related to student achievement, such as classroom assessment scores, student dropout rates, and student responses on motivation surveys. Similarly, with the emphasis in NCLB on improving teacher quality, teacher scores on licensing tests are of interest to researchers.

Researchers also can collect **qualitative data** to measure a dependent variable in an experimental study, but it is far less common, and the data usually are converted to numbers. For example, a study might examine teachers' classroom practices after they participate in a professional development program. The researcher observes the teachers in their classrooms and describes their instructional practices. In an experiment, these practices would be converted to number ratings so that **inferential statistics** could be used to decide whether the teachers in the treatment group are performing better than the teachers in the control group. Numbers are used because the purpose of an experiment is to decide whether something causes an effect. Qualitative narrative descriptions such as "the teacher effectively engaged the class in group discussion" do not lend themselves to an analysis that will lead with high probability to a correct conclusion about the effect of the treatment. Inferential statistics are designed to provide this type of analysis.

Findings

The findings that are of primary interest in experimental research are those that indicate the effects of the independent variable or treatment on the dependent variable; for example, the effects of professional development on teachers' instruction. The success of true experiments and quasi-experiments depends on the extent to which the results lead to unequivocal conclusions about the effectiveness of the treatment or program that was studied. Note that success does not depend on whether the results show positive, negative, or no effects from the treatment, but rather depends on the **validity** of the conclusions about cause and effect, a topic discussed in Chapter Six. Unfortunately, experimental studies that do not demonstrate positive effects of a treatment are of less interest to publishers than those that do. The result is that most reports on experimental studies that find no or negative effects of a program are buried in researchers' and developers' file cabinets. This so-called "file cabinet" problem is detrimental to education because educators need to know both what works and what does not work. One source of such information is education research conferences because conferences tend to be more accepting of reports on various types of findings than are journal publishers.

Descriptive Studies

Research Questions

As the name implies, the purpose of descriptive research is to describe. Descriptive research is designed to answer research questions such as, *What is happening? How is something happening? Why is something happening?*

The following examples illustrate how descriptive research questions might be stated in a report. Note that the research questions are sometimes contained in the form of a statement:

> We were interested in what types of teacher professional development occur in high-performing schools.

How do high-performing schools design professional development?

Do high-performing schools provide teachers with more professional development than low-performing schools?

We hypothesized that teacher professional development has a positive association with student achievement.

Similar to experimental research, descriptive research investigates treatments, that is, education programs, policies, and practices. The critical difference is that in descriptive research, the researcher does not manipulate or vary the treatment. Instead the treatment is studied in its current state. For this reason, descriptive research does not have independent variables.

Participants

In experimental research, research designs are differentiated based on how the participants are assigned to treatment and control groups. In descriptive research, the distinctions among research designs are not apparent. In fact, many sources on research methods do not discuss designs for descriptive research but instead refer to variations based on method of data collection (for example, an **ethnography**) or data analysis (for example, a **regression** study). This primer distinguishes three types of descriptive research designs that differ according to the purpose of the research: **simple descriptive, comparative descriptive,** and **correlational.**

The purpose of a simple descriptive study is to describe the characteristics of a group of participants. The participants can be persons, organizations, settings, or phenomena. Examples are elementary teachers, high schools, rural locations, and classroom assessment practices. In a descriptive study, the researcher does not assign participants to different groups but instead selects them to be in the study because they possess certain characteristics of interest, such as elementary school teacher. The researcher hopes to generate findings that apply to other persons and entities with those same characteristics. The following is an example of a simple descriptive research study:

> A researcher wants to know about the professional development that new teachers experience during their first year of teaching. The researcher administers a survey about professional development to the new teachers in the state and reports on their responses. The researcher describes the type and amount of professional development reported on the survey by the teachers who completed the survey. In this example, the dependent variable is the amount and type of professional development.

There is no independent variable because nothing is varied or manipulated, only described.

The purpose of a comparative descriptive study is to describe and compare the characteristics of two or more groups of participants. The following is an example of a comparative descriptive study:

> A researcher wants to know whether teachers in schools with low-achieving students experience less professional development than teachers in schools with high-performing students. The researcher administers a survey about professional development to the teachers in low- and high-achieving schools in one district. The researcher describes and compares the type and amount of professional development reported on the survey by the teachers in the two types of schools. Again, the dependent variable is the amount and type of professional development, but in this study the findings of interest are the differences in the professional development experienced by teachers in the two types of schools.

The following is an example of an **ex post facto** comparative descriptive study:

> A researcher conducts a study to determine whether teacher professional development is related to increased student achievement. The researcher examines the achievement gains in reading by students of teachers in two schools. In one school the teachers had participated in professional development in reading, while in another school the teachers had no professional development. On face value, this study seems very similar to an experiment. There are two groups with different treatments. The researcher, however, did not select teachers to participate in the two groups. In addition, the researcher did not implement the treatment (the professional development). This type of study is called ex post facto because the research started after the fact; that is, after the professional development occurred. Although this study might be informative, a conclusion that professional development increased student achievement scores would be invalid. *In a descriptive study, the only valid conclusion is about association, not causation.*

The purpose of a correlational study is to describe the statistical association between two or more variables. Correlational research studies differ depending on the number of variables in the study and the type of data analysis. The simplest type of correlational study is **bivariate correlation,** illustrated in the following example:

A researcher wants to know whether teacher professional development (variable 1) is related to student achievement (variable 2). The researcher surveys the state's elementary teachers about the number of hours they spent in professional development last year and obtains the mean student achievement scores for their schools for that academic year. The researcher calculates the correlation between each school's mean teacher professional development hours and mean student achievement scores. The **correlation coefficient** that results from this statistical analysis indicates the strength of the relationship between the two variables, that is, whether professional development has a positive, negative, or no association with student achievement.

Other types of correlational studies are those that use the correlation to predict a result on a dependent variable (that is, **regression**) and those that involve more than two variables (for example, **multiple regression**). Both of these studies are discussed in the Statistics Tutorial in Appendix D.

Data

Depending on the purpose of the research, descriptive studies can collect either quantitative or qualitative data. By necessity, all correlational studies collect quantitative data because numbers are needed to conduct the statistical analyses that produce correlational findings. However, simple descriptive and comparative descriptive studies often collect qualitative data. The following is an example of a simple descriptive study using a **case study** method to collect data:

A researcher wants to know about the implementation of a new three-month teacher professional development program in reading. The researcher conducts a case study of the new program in one elementary school. The researcher observes the professional development classes, reviews program materials, and interviews the teachers and principal. All the findings (primarily narrative descriptions) are analyzed and combined to derive conclusions about how the program was implemented and what teachers and the principal said they learned. If there are multiple schools and hence multiple case studies, the study becomes a comparative descriptive study.

As mentioned in Chapter Three, to many researchers the difference between quantitative and qualitative research is more than the distinction between numbers and narration. Some quantitative researchers view qualitative research as lacking rigor, and some qualitative researchers view quantitative research as artificial. This dichotomy is rooted in philosophical differences that are beyond the scope of this book (interested readers can consult Guba and Lincoln, 1989). For those new to the field of education research, the critical information in evaluating a study is the research question and design, specifically whether a study is asking about a cause or an association and whether it employs an experimental or descriptive design.

Findings

Descriptive studies can produce valid conclusions only about association. As repeated in numerous statistics and research textbooks, *correlation is not causation.* For findings that come from correlational and other descriptive studies, causal statements such as "teacher professional development causes higher/lower student achievement" must be avoided. Related phrases also should be avoided, such as "professional development increases, decreases, works, is effective." Despite this oft-repeated admonition, making claims of causation based on results from descriptive research is a common mistake of interpretation made by researchers, practitioners, and developers of education materials and programs. Unfortunately, such erroneous claims can lead educators to purchase and adopt programs that cannot fulfill their promises.

Some Real Studies

The following are examples of some actual education research studies. Are these studies descriptive or experimental?

1. Allen and Seaman (2004) conducted a study to examine the nature and extent of online education in institutions of higher education. The researchers administered a survey to the chief academic officers of American colleges and universities. Out of 3,068 surveys sent, 1,170 people responded, for a **response rate** of 38 percent. The survey included questions about the different types of online courses each institution offered, the number of online students enrolled at each institution, and the respondents' opinions about student satisfaction with online courses compared to traditional face-to-face courses. The findings indicated that institutions of higher education expect to see a continued growth in online education and student enrollments in online courses. This perception was stronger for private compared to public

institutions. The majority of the institutions said that students were as satisfied with online as traditional courses. Larger institutions were more likely to report that learning outcomes are superior for online compared to traditional courses than were smaller institutions.

2. Riordan and Noyce (2001) investigated the impact of a standards-based mathematics curriculum on the achievement of middle school students. The researchers selected a sample of Massachusetts schools that were implementing the Connected Math Project (CMP), a problem-centered curriculum that is aligned with national mathematics content standards. For comparison purposes, they identified a group of schools that were implementing traditional mathematics curricula and that were similar to the CMP schools in prior student achievement and student socioeconomic status. Students in the CMP schools had performances on the state math assessment that were higher than the students in the comparison schools, a difference that was **statistically significant.**

3. Windschitl and Sahl (2002) studied how middle school teachers learned to use laptop computers for technology instruction in their classrooms. The participants were three teachers in a middle school that had adopted a laptop initiative requiring every student and teacher to have a personal laptop computer for school use. The research questions addressed (1) how teachers' beliefs about learning influenced their integration of instruction with technology, (2) how teachers learned norms and practices related to technology use in the school, and (3) whether a laptop initiative influences teachers to use constructivist pedagogy. The researchers used an "ethnographic perspective" (p. 173) to collect multiple sets of interviews and observations of classes, meetings, and interactions over a two-year period. Overall, the findings indicated that having a strong technology presence in the school did not influence participants' use of technology in instruction, nor did it influence teachers' use of constructivist teaching. Teachers' beliefs about the learning needs of the students at the school and the nature of effective instruction within the school's institutional context influenced the degree to which the teachers integrated the laptop computers with their classroom instruction.

4. Marchant and Paulson (2005) conducted a study to examine the relationship of state high school graduation exams to high school graduation rates and student Scholastic Aptitude Test (SAT) scores.

The researchers first identified states that required a standardized test for graduation, and next they obtained the SAT scores for students from those states. They used **statistical control** to hold constant the influence of other factors that might relate to graduation rates (for example, student poverty). Using multiple regression analysis, the researchers found that requiring a graduation exam has a negative association with a state's mean graduation rates and SAT scores.

Discussion

These four studies illustrate the use of various research methods to answer different research questions. They demonstrate the types of information that specific methods produce. Each method has its own value and utility.

1. The Allen and Seaman (2004) study is comparative descriptive study. It describes online education and compares findings for different types of institutions. Because this is descriptive research, the researchers cannot make any causal claims. For example, the research does not provide evidence that larger institutions produce better online courses.

2. Riordan and Noyce's (2001) study is a quasi-experimental study. Its purpose is to describe the effects of a mathematics curriculum on the achievement of middle school students. The element in the study that makes it experimental research is the use of two student groups, one that receives the mathematics curriculum being investigated (the treatment group) and one that does not (the comparison group). This is a quasi-experimental research design because the students were not randomly assigned to the two groups. However, the comparison group is similar to the treatment group, a characteristic that helps support the validity of the conclusions.

3. The study by Windschitl and Sahl (2002) is a descriptive qualitative study. Its purpose is to describe how teachers learn to use laptop technology in the classroom and the influences on the degree to which teachers integrate technology with instruction. The study makes no claims about the effects of technology but rather provides information on how the interaction of teachers' beliefs can influence technology use in the classroom in the context of an intense technology initiative.

4. The Marchant and Paulson study (2005) is a descriptive correlational study. Its purpose is to describe relationships among the variables of state-required high school graduation exams, graduation rates, and SAT scores. Reports on multiple regression studies can tempt readers to conclude that

causal relationships exist among the variables; for example, that requiring graduation exams causes students to drop out of high school. The use of terms such as *effect* and *impact* can lead readers to erroneous conclusions even when the researcher is careful to avoid them. Regardless of the language used to describe the results and the number of variables that are investigated, correlational research does not support causal claims. However, multiple regression and other types of correlational studies can provide useful information when experimental studies are not possible. (For example, it is not feasible to randomly assign students to different states that have different graduation requirements.)

Chapter 5

Understanding Data Collection in Education Research

IN BOTH experimental and **descriptive** research studies, results and conclusions are based on **data,** which is the factual information gathered as evidence in a study. How data are collected influences whether conclusions about the research are **valid.** This chapter describes three key aspects of data collection: **dependent variables, data-collection instruments,** and **data-collection strategies.**

Dependent Variables

Data are produced by measures of the dependent variables in a study. Student learning and teacher instruction are examples of common dependent variables in education research. A common measure of student learning is achievement tests for which the resulting data are student test scores. A common measure of teacher instruction is classroom observations for which the resulting data are descriptions of classroom practices. The results of a research study are based on analyses of the data produced by measures of the dependent variables.

Before collecting data, the researcher needs to identify and operationally define the dependent variables. An **operational definition** is one that defines a variable based on the methods used to measure it. For example, an operational definition of student learning might be scores on a classroom assessment test. An operational definition of standards-based instruction might be teachers' use of problem-solving assignments in mathematics classes.

Data-Collection Instruments

Data-collection instruments are the tools that researchers use to collect data in research studies. The most commonly used data-collection instruments in education research are **tests, scaled questionnaires, surveys, interviews,** and **observations.**

For research conclusions to be valid, it is important that data-collection instruments have both **validity** and **reliability.** In general, instruments have validity when they measure what they are supposed to measure. For example, results for ninth grade students on a test of algebraic ability should be similar to their results on other tests of algebraic ability (for example, algebra test items used for the Third International Mathematics and Science Study). Instruments are reliable if repeating a measurement within a short time span produces the same result. Another aspect of reliability is whether the items on the instrument that are designed to measure a specific variable actually do so. An extreme example of an unreliable algebra test is one that includes geometry test items because the geometry items would not reliably measure knowledge of algebra. It is the responsibility of the researcher to report data on the validity and reliability of the instruments used for data collection in a study.

Because there are so many things that can vary during a research study, a **pilot test** or a **field test** can increase the probability that measures are appropriate and that conclusions will be valid. Both types of tests refer to trial runs of all or some parts of a study. Data-collection instruments frequently undergo field-testing to establish their validity and reliability. For example, prior to publishing a test, commercial-test developers conduct extensive field-testing. An achievement test for middle school students would be field-tested with students who are in the middle grades and would use the procedures developed for the test, including directions for test administration. The purpose of a field test is to demonstrate that the instrument is valid for its designed use and that the results are reliable.

Tests

With the current emphasis on accountability in education, tests (also known as assessments) are commonly used as data-collection instruments in education research. Most **standardized tests** are produced by commercial-test developers who administer them to large samples of participants via standard procedures. The developers then analyze the results to determine the validity and reliability of the tests. The Scholastic Aptitude Test (SAT) that high school students take prior to college entrance is an example of a standardized test. Reports on research studies that use a commercial test for a study should either summarize the information on validity and reliability or direct the reader to a source for obtaining it.

To judge the validity of conclusions about test results, it is also necessary to know whether the test is **norm-referenced** or **criterion-referenced.** On a norm-referenced test, an individual score is interpreted by comparing it to the scores of a comparison group of persons who took the test. The SAT is an example of a norm-referenced test. An SAT score of 500 was considered average because that was the average score or "norm" of the comparison group of students. The accuracy of score interpretation for norm-referenced tests depends on how similar an individual is to the persons in the comparison group. For example, the SAT would not provide an accurate measure of fifth grade student achievement because the comparison group is entering college freshmen.

On a criterion-referenced test, an individual score is interpreted by comparing it to levels of performance established for the test by professionals in the field that the test addresses. Most of the current standards-based state achievement tests for K–12 students are criterion referenced. This means that test scores are assigned to categories based on the proficiency that students demonstrate in relation to state content standards; for example, categories of unsatisfactory, partially proficient, proficient, and advanced. Another example is the National Assessment of Educational Progress (NAEP), which is also known as "the Nation's Report Card." The U.S. Department of Education has administered the NAEP since 1969 to nationally representative samples of American students in various subject areas, including reading, mathematics, science, writing, U.S. history, civics, geography, and the arts. NAEP scores are reported as the percentages of students who achieve at basic, proficient, and advanced levels, which indicate what students should know and be able to do at the grades assessed, which are grades four, eight, and twelve. (For more information on the NAEP, see http://nces.ed.gov/nationsreportcard/about/.)

Surveys

Technically, a survey is a data-collection method in which participants provide information through self-report. The most common methods of conducting a survey are through questionnaires or interviews, but for most researchers, a survey refers to a questionnaire. Surveys are widely used in education research, particularly in descriptive research studies. The key to a good survey is its design. The survey items should be carefully chosen to produce the data needed to answer the research questions (Dillman, 2000). Survey items should be clear and should not bias a respondent toward particular answers (such as socially desirable responses). When the survey is the main data-collection instrument in a study, the researcher should include the survey in an appendix or make it available upon request.

When a survey is mailed as a questionnaire rather than administered in person, a frequent problem is low **response rate.** Studies that use mailed questionnaires should always report the response rate and discuss the implications if it is low (less than 50 percent). If the response rate is low, the results might not be representative of the group of persons to whom the questionnaire was mailed. It is particularly important to know in a comparative descriptive study whether the response rates were different for the different groups of people who took the survey.

The Schools and Staffing Survey (SASS) is an example of one of the surveys that the U.S. Department of Education administers. The SASS uses four questionnaires: the School Questionnaire, the Teacher Questionnaire, the Principal Questionnaire, and the School District Questionnaire. SASS questionnaires provide information about teacher and administrator characteristics, school programs, general conditions in schools, teacher demand and shortage, and also other topics such as teacher compensation, hiring practices, and student characteristics. The SASS questionnaires have been carefully designed and field tested, and they are periodically reviewed and revised. At the SASS Website (http://nces.ed.gov/surveys/sass/) the public can examine the questionnaires and the individual items and also use them for their own surveys.

The National Center for Education Statistics (NCES), which conducts the SASS and other national education surveys and assessments, has produced many reports on the data collected from SASS, and these are also available at the SASS Website. NCES statistical reports describe the state of education in the United States and are good examples of descriptive research studies. With federal funding, the NCES is able to use sophisticated and systematic sampling and data-collection procedures. The resulting data are of high quality and usually are representative of the **populations** that are sampled. The NCES carefully describes the data obtained from each of its surveys so that those who examine or analyze the data will understand its characteristics and limitations. Many non-NCES researchers conduct studies using NCES data. When a researcher analyzes a data set collected by a different researcher or research organization, the study is referred to as a secondary data analysis. Depending on the research questions, secondary data analyses can be simple descriptive, comparative descriptive, or correlational studies.

Interviews

Interviews are surveys that are administered verbally, either individually or in groups. Structured **interview protocols** ask specific objective questions in a predetermined order. Unstructured interview protocols ask more open-ended questions, and the order often depends on interviewees' answers. Interviews are more **reactive** measures than are paper-and-pencil questionnaires because interviewees often react to the interviewer's verbal and nonverbal responses to what the interviewee has said. This can cause the interviewee to assume that certain responses are desirable. For this reason, interviewers should have training in conducting the interview. This is especially true when more than one interviewer is gathering data. If the interviewers are not asking the questions in the same way, comparisons of data across the interviewees will be invalid. The researcher should describe the interviewer training in the research report and should include the interview protocol in an appendix or provide it upon request.

A **focus group** is a group of participants who are interviewed together and encouraged to share their opinions on a specific topic, which is the focus of the interview. The interviewer (also called the moderator) should have training in conducting this type of interview because adequately and accurately capturing the discussion is not a simple matter.

Scaled Questionnaires

Scaled questionnaires (also called **attitude scales**) are often used to measure attitudes and beliefs. Most scaled questionnaires use a **Likert scale,** in which respondents are given choices reflecting varying degrees of intensity. For example, researchers have developed scaled questionnaires to measure school culture that use items such as those shown in the sidebar.

Scaled questionnaires have the same validity and reliability requirements as tests. For example, a researcher needs to show that a school culture scale is actually measuring culture and not some other property or characteristic of the school, such as material wealth.

To develop a scaled questionnaire, a researcher asks a large sample of participants to respond to a large number of items the researcher has judged to have **content validity** with regard to a particular concept. For example,

---

In this school, staff members are recognized when they do a task well.
Choose one: Strongly disagree, Disagree, Agree, Strongly agree

I feel comfortable about discussing my concerns in this school.
Choose one: Strongly disagree, Disagree, Agree, Strongly agree

the researcher might verify with practitioners and other researchers that the items actually concern aspects of school culture. Next, the researcher often reduces the number of questionnaire items through a statistical procedure called **factor analysis,** which results in a small number of factors that relate to school culture. The researcher might call one factor "staff relations" because it consists of eight items that have to do with staff interactions. In studies where factor analysis has been used, it is important to identify the actual questionnaire items that make up a factor because the name that the researcher gives to the factor might not reflect what was asked of participants. For example, questionnaire items for "staff relations" might ask participants only about interactions with the principal and not about interactions with teachers. It also is important to examine the reliability coefficient for each factor to determine how strongly the questionnaire items that represent a factor are related to one another. A low **reliability coefficient** (less than 0.50) means that the factor is not representative of the questionnaire items.

The data obtained from a scaled questionnaire indicate the strengths of respondents' beliefs about identified factors. For example, assume that the questionnaire items are stated in a positive way (such as, "In this school, staff members are recognized when they do a task well.") and that points are given to each response choice as follows: Strongly disagree, 1; Disagree, 2; Agree, 3; and Strongly agree, 4. A mean score of 1.5 for the factor of "staff relations" would indicate that persons who completed the questionnaire disagreed with statements related to the existence of positive staff relations in their schools.

An example of a scaled questionnaire is the Collective Efficacy Scale (CES) developed by Goddard, Hoy, and Hoy (2000). Goddard and his colleagues have used the CES to study teachers' perceived efficacy in their combined ability to successfully educate the students in their school. In developing the CES, the researchers first showed how the previously researched construct of individual efficacy (Bandura, 1997) could be applied to groups or organizations such as schools. They then identified questionnaire items that would reflect teachers' beliefs about their collective ability as educators. They started with the questionnaire items that Gibson and Dembo (1984) developed to study individual teacher efficacy. For example, the item, "I am able to get through to the most difficult students," on the individual teacher efficacy scale was changed on the CES to, "Teachers in this school can get through to the most difficult students." New questions were developed as well, such as, "The opportunities in this community help ensure that these students will learn." Item development was followed by three tasks designed to establish the validity and reliability of the CES: (1) a review by experts in education and psychology to verify the content validity of the items, (2) a field test by teachers who completed the CES and gave feedback on the clarity and appropriateness of the items, and (3) a pilot study in which teachers took the CES and other scales that measure constructs that should relate to collective efficacy; for example, a scale that measures teachers' trust in colleagues. The results of the pilot study indicated that the CES has validity. For example, collective efficacy was positively related to teachers' trust of their colleagues. The pilot study also demonstrated that the CES has only one factor, that is, all the items are related to a single construct of collective efficacy. The reliability of this one factor was 0.92, indicating that the items on the CES are internally consistent, which means they all measure the same thing—collective efficacy. Finally, the researchers administered the CES to 452 teachers in urban elementary schools and found that collective teacher efficacy was positively associated with student achievement in reading and math.

To demonstrate the usefulness and generalization of the CES, the researchers (Goddard, Logerfo, & Hoy, 2004) asked high school teachers from urban, suburban, and rural school districts to complete the CES. In the results, perceived collective efficacy was the strongest positive predictor of twelfth grade verbal and math–science student achievement on the state test. In addition, higher prior school achievement was positively associated with greater perceived collective efficacy, which the researchers interpreted as a warning for state accountability systems about the effects that negative feedback can have on the beliefs of school faculties. The researchers also suggested that teacher preparation and professional development programs should emphasize skills and attitudes that help teachers believe they can effectively serve all students.

Observations

Observation protocols are instruments used to document observations, usually in classrooms. A good observation protocol has clear operational definitions of the behaviors to be observed, as well as guidelines for recording the frequency of each behavior. For example, an observation protocol for a study of teachers' instructional practices should list the various expected teaching behaviors (such as small-group discussion), provide operational definitions of each behavior (three to six students discussing problems), and indicate the length of each observational period (two hours), as well as the frequency of the observations (two times each week for four weeks). The researcher should provide information about the **inter-rater**

reliability of the observation protocol, which indicates the degree of agreement among the different observers. A reliability rating of 0.90 indicates that the observers agreed 90 percent of the time on their ratings.

Data-Collection Strategies

The strategy used to collect data influences the results of a study. Two main types of data-collection strategies used in education research are **longitudinal** and **cross-sectional.** In a longitudinal study, data are collected from the same participants at different points in time, such as in different years or grades. The purpose is to measure how much the participants change in the dependent variable over time. In a cross-sectional study, data are collected at one point in time from participants who are at different ages or grade levels. The purpose is to draw conclusions about differences in the dependent variable between different participant groups. Each data-collection strategy can be used with either experimental or descriptive research designs.

The following is an example of an experimental cross-sectional research study:

> A researcher randomly assigns second graders, fourth graders, and sixth graders to classes that are either small or large in size. The purpose is to determine whether the difference in year-end student achievement between small and large classes varies depending on the grade levels of the students. In cross-sectional studies, the emphasis is on differences between groups of individuals at one point in time.

The following is an example of a descriptive correlational research study that uses a longitudinal data-collection strategy:

> A researcher studies the relationship between the average class size that each student experienced in grade two and each student's achievement in grades two, four, and six. The purpose is to determine whether the relationship between grade two class size and student achievement remains the same or changes over the four academic years. In longitudinal studies, the emphasis is on individual change over time.

Chapter 6

Issues in Evaluating Education Research

WHEN RESEARCHERS DISCUSS whether findings and conclusions from research can be trusted, they are referring to research **validity.** Researchers have proposed different frameworks for examining validity and use different terms to describe different types of validity (Shadish, Cook, & Campbell, 2002). The terms, however, are not as important as understanding what makes research conclusions valid and knowing what questions to ask about the research. (Although **education research studies** and **evaluation studies** have different goals, procedures, and reporting formats, their conclusions should be assessed with the same criteria for validity.)

Evaluation of Research Validity

Judging the validity of a research study requires some detective work. When a crime is committed, the prosecuting attorney makes arguments to support the conclusion that a person is guilty. The defense attorney presents arguments to support the conclusion that the person is not guilty. Each attorney dissects and analyzes the criminal case. Educators and policymakers who are judging research and evaluation studies need to be like prosecuting attorneys. They need to take apart and analyze studies for possible errors—the "crimes" against research validity (Onwuegbuzie & Daniel, 2003). The researchers are like the defense attorneys. They need to provide evidence they did not commit research crimes. This chapter provides guidance on how to analyze and evaluate an education research or evaluation study.

"Unpacking" or analyzing a research study involves asking four questions:

1. What is the research question?
2. Does the research design match the research question?

3. How was the study conducted?

4. Are there rival explanations for the results?

Answering these questions requires an analysis of the study by using the following steps.

Step 1: Identifying the Research Question

In the introduction to most research reports, the purpose of the study is presented in a **research question** or in a **research hypothesis.** Sometimes the questions are not explicit. Regardless of how a question is phrased, it is important to determine whether the research question is descriptive or causal. *For the research to be valid, it must be designed to answer the type of question asked.*

Experimental research asks whether something causes an effect. The following examples illustrate how causal research questions might be stated in a report. Note that in many reports the word "cause" is not explicit. If the statement or question implies, however, that an effect such as higher student achievement will result from something that is varied such as providing the effect of more versus less teacher professional development, then the research question is a causal question. Again, questions are sometimes given in the form of statements:

We hypothesized that increasing the amount of professional development teachers received would increase student achievement.

We were interested in whether teacher professional development in language arts increases student achievement more than teacher professional development in general teaching strategies.

Does providing teachers with professional development in teaching reading cause their students to have higher achievement in reading?

Experimental research questions in education are also known as "what works" questions. Each of the sample questions is asking whether teacher professional development "works" to improve student achievement. As its name implies, the purpose of the What Works Clearinghouse described in Chapter Two is to produce reports on what interventions work to improve education outcomes, based on research and evaluation studies.

Step 2: Confirming That the Research Design Matches the Research Question

After determining the type of research question that the study addresses, the next step is to examine the **research design.** For research to be valid, the research design must match the research question. Descriptive research questions require **descriptive research designs,** and causal research questions require **experimental research designs.** There are two key features that distinguish descriptive and experimental research designs: (1) the assignment of study participants and (2) the manipulation of an **independent variable.**

For example, a researcher hypothesizes that increasing the amount of professional development teachers receive will increase student achievement. Because this is a causal question, an experimental research design is needed to answer it. Study participants (that is, teachers) should be randomly assigned to two or more **comparison groups** that differ in the amount of professional development (the **treatment**) they receive. One group might receive thirty hours of professional development and a second group ten hours. This is a **true experimental research design** (also called a randomized controlled trial). An alternative is to assign teachers to the professional development groups based on how well the teachers match on characteristics that could influence student achievement. The characteristics used to match the teachers might include years of teaching experience, prior professional development, grade level, and so forth. This is a **quasi-experimental research design.** In both designs, the independent variable in the study is the amount of professional development. The researcher manipulates or varies how much professional development the teachers will receive.

In another example, a researcher hypothesizes that teacher professional development has a positive association with student achievement. This is a descriptive research question, so a descriptive research design is needed, specifically a **correlational research design** because the question concerns association. The researcher surveys the elementary teachers in a school district concerning how many hours of professional development they received last year and measures the statistical association between professional development hours and the mean achievement scores of their students. This is not an experimental research design because teachers are not assigned to different comparison groups and the researcher does not manipulate or vary the amount of professional development (the treatment) that teachers receive.

In both examples, the research design matches the research question. In general, the greatest concern for validity is when a research study appears to seek a causal connection but does not use an experimental research design. A correlational research design would not be a valid way to determine whether increasing the amount of professional development teachers receive increases student achievement. It lacks participant assignment and the manipulation of a treatment. In the absence of these two elements, the most that descriptive research can uncover is the correlation or association of factors; it cannot reveal an actual causal relationship. Correlation indicates that two or more factors occur in association with one another; it does not indicate whether one factor causes another.

Step 3: Examining How the Study Was Conducted

Step 3 concerns the **research method,** which refers to how the study was conducted and how the research design was implemented. A research report should provide enough details about the method so the study can be **replicated.** Without these details, it is difficult and sometimes impossible to judge the validity of the research.

Four key components of the research method influence research validity: the participants, the treatment, data collection, and data analysis.

Participants and Selection

The research report should describe the number of participants in the study, as well as their characteristics. This description should include not only the characteristics of persons, but also those of entities such as schools and districts. Look for characteristics that could influence the results, such as the following:

- Student characteristics—Grade level, gender, socioeconomic status, ethnicity, language status (for example, second language learner), prior student achievement

- Teacher (classroom) characteristics—Experience, grade level, class size, subject area, preparation, certification status

- School characteristics—Number of students, teachers, paraprofessionals, administrators, and other certified staff; location; grade levels; socioeconomic status of students; ethnicity of students; mean student achievement data

- District characteristics—Number and grade levels of schools; number of students; number and types of teachers, administrators, and other certified staff; location; community characteristics

The study should also describe how the participants were selected for the study **sample.** Most researchers do not have the luxury of selecting a **random sample** from a **population** of participants. An exception is the U.S. Department of Education, which conducts random sampling to collect education survey data. If the sample is not random, conclusions about the population based on the sample can be erroneous. With a nonrandom sample, valid conclusions can be made only about the sample of participants in the study.

A related issue is how participants were assigned to the different comparison groups in the study. Without **random assignment, selection bias** can occur. For example, if a researcher selected teachers to participate in one of two types of professional development based on school location, the results could be influenced by characteristics of the schools rather than the professional development.

Definition, Description, and Implementation of Treatment

The treatment refers to the program, policy, or practice that is being studied. Treatments are often **interventions** of some type such as a special reading program for low-achieving students, a type of teacher preparation, or a mathematics curriculum designed to improve practices or conditions. In an experimental research study, the treatment is the independent variable. Researchers should provide the **operational definition** of the treatment being studied. In addition, the definition should have **construct validity.**

For example, in a study of teacher professional development, an operational definition of the treatment could be a class in literacy instruction that teachers attend after school two times each week. Most educators would probably agree that this treatment is a valid example of professional development. If the operational definition were that teachers go out to lunch twice a week, most educators would object to calling this professional development. The treatment should be defined in a way that is a valid example or representation of the construct being studied; in this case, professional development. It is important to always determine the operational definition of the treatment in a study. Many research claims are invalid because the actual treatment in the study has been mislabeled.

Some treatments in education are particularly difficult to define. For example, researchers define teacher content knowledge (for instance, knowledge of mathematics) in various ways, such as the number of college courses the teacher completed in a subject area, whether the teacher earned a college major or minor in a subject, and the teacher's scores on teacher licensing tests. All these measures are **proxy** measures for the actual knowledge teachers have about a particular content area. When a proxy measure is used, valid conclusions can be made only about the measure and not about the construct the measure represents (in this case, actual knowledge).

In addition to a valid definition, the treatment must be implemented consistently. Researchers should report measures that demonstrate **treatment fidelity.** Did the treatment occur as planned? If the treatment is a professional development class in literacy instruction, the researcher should report information and data that demonstrate the class occurred as planned. This might include participant attendance, content of the instruction, class schedule, and class activities. In addition, if any event occurred during the treatment that might influence the results—for example, a literacy conference that some of the teachers attended during the study—it should be reported. The literacy conference might interact with the professional development, making the treatment appear to be more effective than it was.

The Data and How They Are Collected

Empirical research studies collect information about something that can be observed in the real world or in the laboratory. This factual information is referred to as **data.** Data make up the body of information produced by measures of the **dependent variable(s)** in a study. Student achievement and teacher classroom practices are common dependent variables in education research. Corresponding examples of data are student test scores and classroom observations. How data are collected influences whether conclusions about the research are valid. Two important considerations are the data-collection instruments and the data-collection procedures.

Chapter Five describes the most commonly used data-collection instruments in education research: **tests, scaled questionnaires** (attitude scales), **surveys, interviews,** and **observations.** To evaluate a research study, it is necessary to know whether the data-collection instruments have validity and **reliability.** There should be evidence that an instrument measures what it is supposed to measure (validity) and that if the measurement is repeated within a short time span, a similar result will be obtained (reliability). For example, if a test of teachers' knowledge of pedagogy is valid, it should be correlated with other measures of pedagogy, such as lesson plans. If the test is reliable, the results should be similar if a teacher takes the test or answers similar test items twice within three weeks.

Another concern related to the validity of data-collection instruments is how the instruments are used. A test that is a valid measure of algebraic ability might not be a valid measure of the ability to teach algebra. If a test is used in a research study for a purpose that the test was not intended, then the scores will not be a valid measure of the dependent variable. A scaled questionnaire developed to measure school culture might not have any relationship to leadership or student achievement, yet sometimes a researcher will make such unwarranted conclusions. The conclusions of a research study can be invalid despite the use of a valid data-collection instrument if the conclusions extend beyond the limits of what was measured. In general, the name of an instrument does not necessarily ensure that it is a valid measure of what its name suggests. For example, an instrument called a "Test of Teacher Content Knowledge" is not necessarily a test that actually measures teacher content knowledge.

Data-collection procedures refer to exactly how and when the data were collected. The procedures used to collect data influence the results, so it is important that the procedures be carefully designed and described in research reports. For example, whether or not survey respondents are guaranteed anonymity affects whether they are honest in their responses to the surveys. The time and frequency of classroom observations influence the type of data obtained from the observations. A classroom observation conducted the day before spring break is unlikely to provide valid data about a teacher's instruction. In experimental studies, it is critical that the same data-collection procedures be used for the treatment and comparison groups. If the procedures are different, then the groups will differ in more ways than just the presence or absence of a treatment. Consequently, the study results could be due to either the variation in data collection or the treatment, or both.

Data Analysis

When evaluating whether or not a research or evaluation study did a good job of analyzing the data it produced, it is important to distinguish between **quantitative data** and **qualitative data.**

Quantitative Data Analysis. Researchers analyze quantitative data through **statistics.** The wide availability of statistical software programs makes it easy for researchers to analyze data, but also makes it easy to use statistics incorrectly, leading to invalid research conclusions.

The computation of **inferential statistics** is the primary basis for research conclusions about a treatment effect; that is, that a treatment or intervention worked. A **statistically significant** effect at the 0.05 level means that there is a 5 percent or less probability that the result occurred by chance. By convention, social scientists have chosen this percentage as the cut-off point (although other percentages are sometimes chosen). Thus, when there is statistical significance, the researcher concludes that the treatment effect did not occur by chance but occurred due to the treatment that was implemented. Researchers should not discuss nonsignificant results (results with a probability of occurrence that is greater than 5 percent) as though they indicate real treatment effects or group differences.

The probability of detecting a statistically significant effect increases with the size of the sample. There are two consequences of this relationship. First, a treatment effect might not be detected in a research study with a small **sample size** (for example, fewer than thirty participants). As a result, the researcher's conclusion that the treatment has no effect might be invalid. Second, with a large sample size, a very small treatment effect can be statistically significant, but the **practical significance** of the treatment might be limited; in other words, not enough of an effect to justify its adoption into a program. For this reason, the researcher should report the **effect size** of the treatment. The effect size is a measure of the amount of difference between a treatment group and a control group that did not receive the treatment. The larger the effect size, the larger the effect of the treatment on the outcome.

The concept of **error** is at the heart of inferential statistics. The more error that occurs in a study, the more the scores will vary. The more **variability** there is, the less likely it is that a treatment effect will be detected. Think of error and variability as background noise and the treatment as a sound. When there is too much noise, some sounds cannot be detected. Error in a research study can occur due to small sample sizes, unsystematic treatment implementation, and unreliable measurement. The researcher should report the efforts made to standardize the treatment and the measurement, such as **pilot-testing** the treatment and training the data collectors.

For a deeper understanding of these and other statistical concepts, see the Statistics Tutorial in Appendix D.

Qualitative Data Analysis. In **qualitative research,** the data consist of narrative descriptions and observations. Although statistics are not used, qualitative data analyses need to be systematic to support valid research conclusions. Organization is at the heart of qualitative data analyses. In most qualitative research studies, large amounts of descriptive information are organized into categories and themes through coding. **Coding** is designed to reduce the information in ways that facilitate interpretations of the findings. A report on qualitative research should give detailed descriptions of the codes and the coding procedures. The following is an example of coding qualitative data:

> A researcher interviews the principals of ten elementary schools to answer the following research question: *What challenges do schools face when adopting a comprehensive school reform model?* The researcher reads the transcriptions of the interviews and lists all the topics that the ten interviews addressed. Next the researcher groups similar topics into categories such as parent approval, teacher collaboration, and time issues. The researcher uses these categories to code each interview and then assembles the information for each coded category across the ten interviews. The researcher can then describe, for example, the degree to which parent approval was a challenge for the interviewed principals.

The concept of error also is applicable to qualitative research studies. To minimize error, qualitative researchers need to maintain careful records of their field notes and observations. For this reason, interviews are often tape-recorded and transcribed.

Step 4: Detecting Rival Explanations for the Results

At the end of a research report, the researcher presents conclusions based on the results that were obtained through the study. To judge whether a conclusion can be trusted, always ask this question: *Could there be an explanation for the results other than the conclusion reached?* Researchers refer to these **rival explanations** as **threats to validity** because they threaten the validity of the research conclusions (Shadish et al., 2002). It is the job of the researcher to rule out rival explanations by demonstrating that they do not apply to the study.

Quantitative Research

It is especially important to identify or rule out rival explanations when the researcher concludes that a treatment (for example, an education program or intervention) has an effect—in other words, that something works. There are several common factors that account for rival explanations in quantitative studies of the effectiveness of an intervention, that is, in experimental research studies.

Selection bias concerns how the study participants are assigned to treatment and **control groups** in a study. Random assignment is the best way to ensure that student and teacher characteristics that might influence outcomes do not systematically favor the treatment or the control group. Random assignment of students and teachers sometimes is not feasible, however. To rule out a rival explanation due to selection bias, the researcher should describe the characteristics of both groups of teachers and their students (that is, in the control group and the treatment group) and either show how the comparison groups are similar or conduct data analyses that **statistically control** for individual student characteristics (for example, socioeconomic status) and teacher characteristics (such as teaching experience).

Sample attrition (also called **mortality**) can be a rival explanation. If more participants (for example, teachers or students) leave the treatment group than the control group (or vice versa), the results could be due to differences in characteristics between the groups at the **posttest** that did not exist at the **pretest.** To rule out a rival explanation based on sample attrition, the researcher should document who left the study and why. Sample attrition is a particular concern in **longitudinal research** studies where the same participants are studied over a long time span. The participants who remain in the study could have different characteristics than those who left.

Treatment diffusion or spillover, another rival explanation, can occur when participants who are in different comparison groups operate in the same environment, such as teachers in the same school. Teachers in the control group might overhear treatment teachers discussing the intervention, or control teachers might gain access to materials being used for the intervention. The researcher should ask participants in each group about their interactions and document their responses.

History effects can be a problem in research studies that occur over a long time, such as a year or more. For example, there might be a change in school leadership. To rule out rival explanations based on history effects, the researcher needs to monitor all possible occurrences and demonstrate they do not influence the results of the treatment and control groups differently.

Practice effects refer to a rival explanation that results from **repeated measures** of the same individuals. In any research study where participants are tested or measured more than once, there is a possibility that the participants' responses on the second and subsequent tests are affected by practice on the pretest. Practice effects are less likely to occur when there are longer time spans between the pretest and posttest. The researcher should determine whether participants practiced for the posttest, and especially whether practice occurred more in the treatment group compared to the control group. (Test practice by students for state assessments has become commonplace.)

Regression toward the mean is a rival explanation that can occur when participants have extremely low or extremely high scores on a pretest. Extreme scores tend to move toward the average or mean score when a test is repeated. This means that extreme scorers will score less extremely on posttests, even without a treatment. To rule out this rival explanation, the researcher should demonstrate, for example, that the students of the treatment and control teachers do not differ in the proportion of extreme scorers.

Qualitative Research

The main validity concern in qualitative research is the credibility of the results (Creswell, 2002). Qualitative researchers use **verification methods** to support their conclusions. For example, through **triangulation** of results, information from different measures in the study, such as interviews and documents, converges to support an interpretation. **Member checking** involves reporting the results of data analyses (that is, the categories and themes) to the participants to verify that the researcher's interpretations are correct. A researcher also can verify findings by conducting a deliberate search for **disconfirming evidence,** which is information that does not fit the categories, themes, and interpretations.

Researcher and Participant Effects

Both quantitative and qualitative research studies are subject to rival explanations from researcher and participant effects. This is particularly true of studies that involve interaction between a researcher or evaluator and a participant.

Researcher bias occurs when a researcher's or evaluator's expectations concerning study outcomes influence the results. In qualitative studies, researcher bias can influence researchers to code and interpret qualitative data such as interview responses in ways consistent with expectations. In quantitative studies, researchers can communicate their expectancies to the participants and influence how the participants respond to an intervention.

Participant reactivity refers to the tendency of participants to react in different ways based on the research context. For example, students might improve their reading achievement not because of the characteristics of a reading intervention but because the treatment they received made them feel special and increased their motivation to perform well. Another type of reactivity is some participants' need to appear socially desirable. This reaction creates problems for survey and interview studies because the participants might not answer truthfully.

Researchers should indicate how their data collection and analysis procedures rule out rival explanations due to researcher and participant effects. The use of multiple verification methods can minimize researcher bias in qualitative data analysis. The use of **blind** data collectors who are unaware of the treatment condition or research hypothesis can **control** for researcher bias in experimental research studies. In studies of interventions, control groups can participate in an activity unrelated to the intervention, such as an extra recess. Questions on surveys and interviews can be designed to avoid socially desirable responding. Some surveys and attitude scales include questions that assess whether participants are lying, such as, "Have you ever told a lie?" When persons answers no, it is likely they are lying on this and possibly other questions.

Evaluation of the Scientific Characteristics of Education Research

The purpose for "unpacking" a research or evaluation study is to evaluate the trustworthiness of the findings and the validity of the research conclusions. The National Research Council's Guiding Principles for Scientific Research (2002), described in Chapter Two, suggests other important considerations in evaluating a research study. As indicated in Exhibit 6.1, scientific Principles 3 and 4 concern research validity issues similar to those addressed by the four steps in unpacking a research study described in this chapter. Principles 1 and 2 concern the importance of the research question and its relation to prior knowledge and theory. Principle 5 addresses the potential of research findings for replication and **generalization,** criteria that are especially important when evaluating the usefulness of a study, which is discussed in greater detail in Chapter Ten. Principle 6 stresses the need for research studies to undergo **peer review.** Through careful reading and analysis of a study report, it is possible to determine whether the study followed the six principles of scientific inquiry. The guiding questions in Exhibit 6.1 can be used for this analysis.

EXHIBIT 6.1

Guiding Questions About Scientific Principles in Education Research

Scientific Principle

1. Pose significant questions that can be investigated empirically.

Guiding Questions

What is the research question?

Will answering the research question provide new knowledge or solve a problem?

Is it possible to answer the research question through observations of some type?

Scientific Principle

2. Link research to relevant theory.

Guiding Questions

What theory or framework is being used to answer the research question?

What is the relationship between the theory or framework and the way that the study is being conducted?

Scientific Principle

3. Use methods that permit direct investigation of the question.

Guiding Questions

What methods were used to conduct the study?

Does the study indicate how the method is appropriate for the research question?

Is there detailed information on how the method was carried out so other researchers can repeat the study?

Does the study report on the validity and reliability of the measuring instruments?

Does the study describe potential problems with the method used?

Scientific Principle

4. Provide a coherent and explicit chain of reasoning.

Guiding Questions

Does the study rule out explanations for the results other than the explanation given by the researcher?

Does the study demonstrate how errors or threats to the validity of the results were avoided?

Scientific Principle

5. Replicate and generalize across studies.

Guiding Questions

Is there sufficient information to repeat the study?

Are there other studies that have found similar results but in different settings or with different participants?

What additional research is needed to extend and generalize the results of the study?

Scientific Principle

6. Disclose research to encourage professional scrutiny and critique.

Guiding Questions

Where has the study been published?

Has the study been reviewed by other education researchers?

Chapter 7

Evaluating Experimental Research Studies

CHAPTER SIX DISCUSSES the general issues to consider when evaluating education research studies. When considering these issues, the criteria will differ depending on the type of research. This chapter demonstrates the criteria for evaluating **experimental research** studies.

The two examples that follow are synopses of experimental studies reported in the education research literature. In reality, evaluating a research study requires a review of the entire research report. However, for the purposes of this primer, a summary is used to provide the essential information in a study, and additional details are provided in the analysis of the study. The citations for the original reports are available in the References section at the back of the book so interested readers can obtain the reports and read them in their entirety. (There are tips on reading research reports in Appendix A.)

Evaluation of a True Experimental Research Study

As described in Chapter Three, a **true experimental research design,** also called a randomized controlled trial (RCT), involves the following elements: (1) a **treatment** is administered (the **independent variable**) and its effects are measured on a **dependent variable**; (2) participants are **randomly assigned** to different groups that receive varied amounts of the treatment. The groups frequently include a **control group** in which the participants receive no treatment. Some researchers refer to the true experimental research design as the "gold standard" for determining whether a treatment causes an effect. However, for an experiment to produce findings that support valid causal conclusions, it needs to possess several critical characteristics. By assessing experimental studies for these characteristics, it is possible to determine the **validity** of their findings and conclusions.

*True Experimental Study: Effects of Intensive Reading
Remediation for Second and Third Graders and a
One-Year Follow-up*

The purpose of this study by Blachman, Schatschneider, Fletcher, and others (2004) was "to evaluate the effectiveness of an intensive reading intervention for second- and third-grade children with reading disabilities who were selected on the basis of poor word-level skills" (p. 444). The researchers wanted to investigate whether an intervention could improve the word skills of struggling early readers and whether improvements would endure after one year. Children were selected for the study from eleven schools based on teacher ratings of reading difficulties and low scores on a reading test. Within the identified pool of poor readers, the children were randomly assigned to either the treatment or control group. The treatment involved daily one-to-one tutoring in reading for fifty minutes, five days each week for one academic year. Each tutoring lesson had several steps designed to help the children understand phonetic connections, develop fluency and comprehension skills, and enjoy text-based reading. The children in the control group received their usual classroom reading instruction and any normally scheduled remedial instruction provided by their schools. All the children were **pretested** prior to the intervention and **posttested** afterwards via several different reading tests. The results indicated **statistically significant** differences favoring the treatment group on all reading and spelling posttest measures at the end of the school year. In addition, the treatment children had a significantly greater growth rate on the reading measures than the control children. The treatment group continued to outperform the control group one year after the treatment ended. However, the two groups did not significantly differ in growth rate during the follow-up year.

Research Question

In the example, as frequently happens in research studies, the **research question** is not stated in the form of a question but rather is given in a statement about the purpose. The purpose of the study is to evaluate the effectiveness of a reading intervention (p. 444). In other words, does the intervention work? Does it cause an effect on reading achievement?

Research Design

Because the research question is about cause and effect, an experimental **research design** is needed to answer it. The information needed to identify whether the researchers used an experimental design first becomes apparent in the method section of the report (p. 446). The use of a random method to assign the children to treatment or control groups indicates that this is a true experimental or RCT study.

Participants

All research reports should describe the participants in the study and how they were selected. Reports on experimental research studies should demonstrate that there was no **selection bias** that might influence the results.

In the example, the researchers describe the extensive process they used to select the children for the study (pp. 445–446). First teachers identified children they rated as having low reading skills. The researchers then sought permission from over seven hundred families to further test the children, with 42 percent granting permission. (The researchers indicated that the granting of permission was not related to the socioeconomic status of the family.) These children were then screened via standardized reading and intelligence tests. Children who were above the reading cutoff and below the intelligence cutoff were eliminated from the study. Reasons for eliminating additional children were fully explained (for example, neurological disorder, too old, the need to have an equal proportion of boys and girls in the treatment and control groups). The remaining children were randomly assigned to the treatment or control group within each school, grade, and gender. (This assured that the treatment group did not by chance favor one school, grade, or gender.) Of the forty-eight children originally assigned to the treatment group, eleven were excluded for various reasons that the researchers documented (for example, a heart condition, moved to a different school). Of the forty-one children originally assigned to the control group, nine were excluded for reasons that included the reluctance of parents who did not want their children to participate if they did not receive the tutoring treatment. The researchers reported that the treatment and control children did not differ in age, mother's educational level, the screening tests, or absences during the treatment and follow-up years. In addition, there was no **sample attrition**—no loss of participants from either group during the two years of the study.

The extensive documentation that the researchers provide about the study participants and the demonstration of group equality prior to the start of the treatment is evidence that the study does not have a selection bias that favors one of the two groups. This study is an excellent example of ruling out **rival explanations** related to participant selection.

Treatment

It is especially important that reports on experiments describe the treatment in detail by providing **operational definitions** of the treatment and its components. If something is effective, then others will want to use it, and without details, they will not be able to **replicate** the treatment.

The report for this experimental study describes the procedures used to deliver the treatment to the children, the instruction that the tutors delivered, and the qualifications and training of the tutors (pp. 448–450). The researchers reported that treatment children received an average of 105 hours of tutoring (a measure of treatment intensity). Tutors were certified teachers, and they completed a forty-five-hour training session (also described) prior to beginning their tutoring of the treatment children. Each tutoring session consisted of a five-step lesson based on a framework used for preventing reading problems. The lessons used a common set of materials and texts (described in the report), but lessons also were individualized for students.

Treatment fidelity is critical to the validity of experimental research. Was the treatment implemented as planned? The researchers report several measures of treatment fidelity (p. 450). Researchers observed lessons and rated the degree to which they included the five required steps. They also reviewed tutors' lessons and audiotaped lessons. These ratings and observations were conducted independently by two or more persons and then later examined for agreement, which was close to 100 percent.

Another consideration is what participants in the control group were doing while the treatment was being implemented. It is a misconception that those in a control group are not receiving a treatment. They are doing something, which should be documented by the experimenter. The researchers describe the reading instruction that children in the control group received during the treatment year (p. 250). Some of the control children received remedial instruction through their normal school programs. This occurrence could work against finding effects of the treatment because some of the control children received aspects of the reading treatment and they might also increase their reading skills (an effect similar to **treatment diffusion**). However, the researchers indicate that these control children did not significantly differ on the pretests and posttests from the control children who did not receive remedial instruction.

Data-Collection Instruments and Procedures

As discussed in Chapter Five, the instruments and procedures used to collect **data** influence the validity of the research findings. The validity and **reliability** of **data-collection instruments** should be documented, and procedures for collecting data should be the same for the different participant groups.

The researchers describe in detail the data-collection instruments they use and the reasons for using them (pp. 446–448). They list a battery of three reading tests and one mathematics test and a reading skills battery with nine component tests. The report provides the source of each test (that is, name, publication, and date) and the reliability of each test. (Presumably the test publisher can provide information on the validity of the test.) Together the tests took one hour and forty-five minutes to administer, and the tests were given multiple times over the two years of the study. Scores on these tests constitute the dependent variables in the study, although the researchers refer to them as "measures" (p. 446).

Regarding data-collection procedures, "All testers were extensively trained in the administration and scoring of both batteries, retrained before each wave of testing, and blind to the condition of the children" (p. 447). In other words, the data collectors were highly trained and were not aware of whether the children were in the treatment or control group. Training of data collectors controls for possible errors in the data due to the use of incorrect procedures. If these errors occur more for one group than for another, differences might be due to data-collection errors and not the treatment. The use of data collectors who are not conducting the study and who are **blind** to the group assignment of those they are testing is a good way to avoid **researcher bias**.

Data Analysis and Results

Sophisticated experimental studies such as this example often use sophisticated **inferential statistics** to analyze the results and establish statistical significance. However, good reports make these results accessible to the readers, including those who are not well versed in the specific statistics reported.

Blachman et al. (2004) describe the statistics they chose and the reason for their choice. Their primary way to estimate the effects of the reading treatment was through an analysis of covariance (ANCOVA). This statistical approach is similar to an **analysis of variance** (**ANOVA**). The main difference is that in a **repeated measures** study, ANCOVA controls for the influence of the first measure (that is, the pretest) on the second measure (the posttest). In this study, children's reading performance on the pretest could influence their performance on the posttest. This could threaten the validity of the research if the children in the treatment group had higher pretest scores than the children in the control group. ANCOVA adjusts the posttest scores for the influence of the pretest so that the adjusted posttest scores are not biased due to the pretest. ANCOVA is a method of **statistically controlling** for **extraneous variables** (variables other than the treatment that might influence the results).

The treatment and control children in the study were not significantly different on any of the pretest measures. However, on the posttest, the treatment children had significantly higher scores on all reading measures than the control children. This result indicates the treatment had a positive effect on reading that was more than would be expected by chance. (For $p < 0.05$, only five times out of a hundred would such a result occur by chance.) The researchers report **effect sizes** ranging from $d = 1.69$ to $d = 0.55$ for the different reading measures. The effect size statistics indicate that on average, treatment children scored from 1.69 to 0.55 standard deviations higher than the control children. However, the researchers do not provide any guidance to the readers on how to interpret this effect size. They probably assume that those reading the report are familiar with the conventional interpretation of a 0.50 effect size as "medium" and 1.00 as "large." (See the Statistical Tutorial in Appendix D for an explanation of effect sizes.)

Rival Explanations

It is the job of researchers to demonstrate that rival explanations do not apply to their studies. They need to show that there are no explanations for the results other than the conclusions reached. If there are other explanations, these should be acknowledged and described.

Blachman et al. demonstrate the avoidance of rival explanations through their use of systematic procedures throughout the study. Their participant selection and assignment processes avoid the threat of selection bias. They carefully document the number of participants excluded from the study and note the lack of sample attrition. The documentation of treatment fidelity of the tutoring in the treatment group and of the nature of the instruction received by the control group provide some evidence that **history effects** were avoided. The use of trained data collectors who were unaware or blind to group assignment helped avoid researcher bias. **Practice effects** (that is, from pretest to posttest) were controlled to some degree by the use of a statistical procedure that adjusted for pretest scores. They do not discuss

regression to the mean (that is, low scores that become higher on a second testing), which was controlled for by the use of random assignment from a group of children who were all low scorers.

In the discussion of the results, the researchers provide evidence that other rival explanations specific to their study do not apply. The researchers note that the treatment children received their reading instruction in smaller groups and had more hours of instruction than the control children. However, the researchers demonstrate that within the control group, there was no relationship between the size of the instructional group and reading scores. In addition, the control students who received more hours of instruction performed similarly to those who received fewer hours. The researchers acknowledge that both group size and hours of instruction should be controlled for in future studies.

One possible rival explanation that the researchers do not address concerns an aspect of the treatment condition that they mention. Specifically, children in the treatment condition were part of another study that involved neuroimaging and required three out-of-state trips, presumably with their parents (p. 446). It is possible that this "special treatment" influenced their motivation to perform, a type of **participant reactivity.**

Scientific Characteristics

In addition to having trustworthy findings that can support valid conclusions, to be scientific, research studies should link with prior research and theory, have the potential for replication and generalization, and be peer reviewed (National Research Council, 2002).

In the introduction to their research report, Blachman et al. review prior research on reading (pp. 444–445). They note the preponderance of research on prevention of reading difficulties, and they stress the need for additional research on how to help readers who currently are struggling. The wealth of details the researchers provide about study implementation make the potential for replication and **generalization** fairly high. The one stumbling block might be the special neuorimaging assessments that treatment children underwent, which would not be an aspect of future studies of the reading program. An issue that is indirectly related to generalization is that of cost. The reported effect sizes indicate that the study has **practical significance,** but a cost-benefit analysis is needed to determine whether reading gains are sufficient to justify the cost of program adoption by schools. With regard to **peer review,** the *Journal of Educational Psychology,* the journal in which the study was published, requires stringent peer review prior to publication. Information on the nature of the peer review is available in the journal.

Evaluation of a Quasi-experimental Research Study

The main difference between a true experimental and a **quasi-experimental research design** is the way in which participants are assigned to treatment and comparison groups. In a quasi-experimental study, an intact group of participants receive a treatment, and they are compared to a different group of participants who do not receive the treatment. For example, a third grade class is participating in a special mathematics curriculum. Their scores on a mathematics achievement test are compared to those of a third grade class that is not participating in the special curriculum.

In a quasi-experimental study, participants are not individually assigned to the treatment or control groups. This characteristic makes quasi-experimental studies subject to selection bias because the results might be due to the treatment or to the characteristics of the participants who happen to be in the treatment group. For example, a third grade class is likely to consist of students who are in the class for a variety of reasons: recommendation of the previous teacher, parent request, pairs of friends, assignment of learning disabled children to one classroom, and so forth. These preexisting differences between treatment and control classes can influence the results on the dependent variable (for example, an achievement test). Random assignment to treatment and comparison groups prevents systematic influences from these individual differences occurring because chance procedures are used to assign the students to the groups. Each student has an equal chance of being assigned to a class, so students with specific characteristics end up in a particular class no more than would be expected by chance. A caveat is that for purposes of equating participant groups, random assignment works better with larger **sample sizes.**

Researchers often use **matching** in quasi-experimental research designs, a procedure in which a control group is chosen based on its similarity to the treatment group in characteristics related to the dependent variable. For third grade mathematics achievement, such characteristics might include gender, prior achievement in mathematics, and socioeconomic status. The closer the match between the treatment and the control group, the lower is the probability that selection bias will threaten the validity of the results.

> *Quasi-experimental Study: The Effects of Mandatory, Competitive Science Fairs on Fifth Grade Students' Attitudes Toward Science and Interests in Science*
>
> The purpose of this study by Blenis (2000) was to examine the influences of science fair participation and awards on elementary school students' interests in attitudes toward science. Two elementary schools were chosen for the study based on the willingness of

the principals to have the schools participate and based on the requirement to have at least four fifth-grade classes in each school. The independent variables were the type of student participation in the science fair (mandatory or voluntary) and the type of awards given to students who completed science fair projects (competitive or noncompetitive). Within each school, the researcher randomly assigned each fifth grade class to one of four research groups: (1) mandatory-competitive, (2) mandatory-noncompetitive, (3) voluntary-competitive, and (4) voluntary-noncompetitive. The science fairs were implemented within each classroom over a period of six weeks. The teachers were trained on the general topic of science fairs and on implementing the research study. In the mandatory groups, teachers told the students they were required to complete an experiment and document it in a science project notebook. Teachers in the voluntary groups only encouraged student participation and discussed the benefits of participation. In the competitive groups, teachers told the children that the top two projects would receive medals, while students in the noncompetitive groups were told that all participants would receive a ribbon. The children were instructed to complete their projects outside of school time and to do the work primarily on their own. All students completed pretests and posttests of their interests in and attitudes toward science. Because only five students chose to participate voluntarily, the data for the voluntary groups could not be analyzed. The results for the two mandatory groups indicated that type of reward did not significantly influence students' *attitudes* toward science but did significantly influence students' *interests* toward science. Students in the noncompetitive group had higher interest scores than those in the competitive group. In addition there was a statistically significant interaction between the two independent variables. Students with low initial interests on the pretest who were in the noncompetitive group experienced a greater increase in interest on the posttest compared to the initially low students in the competitive group. The researcher concluded that competition in a science fair might not benefit all students and that award structures in elementary school science fairs should be reexamined.

Research Question

As in the first example, the research question is given in a statement: "The current study examined the relationships between participation in science fairs, the award structure of science fairs, interests in science, and attitudes toward science for elementary schools students" (p. 3). The report also out-lines the **research hypotheses** that are being tested (p. 4). The main hypoth-esis is that competitive awards and mandatory participation would be associated with lower student scores in science interest and attitude com-pared to scores for noncompetitive awards and voluntary participation. An additional hypothesis is that reward structure and type of participation would interact in their influence on student interest and attitude scores. Finally, more students were expected to volunteer for a science fair with noncompetitive awards than with competitive awards.

Research Design

Although the researcher does not use causal language to describe the study, the research hypotheses imply cause and effect and indicate that an experi-mental research design should be used. In the method section, the researcher indicates that within each of the two schools, the four fifth-grade classes were randomly assigned to one of the four treatment groups (p. 8). This resulted in one class per treatment in each school for a total of eight classes, two per treatment group. Although random assignment was used, this is not a true experimental study. The reason is that the unit of analysis is the individual student, but students were not randomly assigned to the different treatment groups. Instead, intact classes were randomly assigned to the treat-ment groups. The design for this study is therefore quasi-experimental. How-ever, the researcher does not make this explicit in the method section, although the study is described as quasi-experimental in the study **abstract.**

Participants

The participants in the study are fifth grade students in a Florida school dis-trict. In the method section, the researcher describes the race and gender characteristics of all the fifth grade students in the district and of the 216 students in the study (pp. 8–9). In addition, the total number of gifted and learning disabled children in the study sample is specified. However, the report does not compare student characteristics for the four treatment groups. This missing information is critical because the results might be due to student differences and not the type of treatment. Without information on the participants in each of the groups, it is impossible to rule out selec-tion bias as a **threat to validity.** Although the random assignment of treat-ments to classes might control for differences among classes in the same school, it does not control for students' individual differences. As the researcher notes, "The students at each school were already placed in their classes" (p. 9). Possibly a better method of treatment assignment in this study would be to balance the distribution of treatments among the classes such that no one treatment has a preponderance of students with characteristics that might influence the results, such as learning disabled students. An additional characteristic that could be considered in assigning treatments is students' prior achievement in science. The author even suggests that attitude toward science, one of the dependent variables, is related to science achievement.

Treatment

Blenis provides clear operational definitions of the four treatments (p. 4) and describes details of treatment implementation (p. 11). Teachers participated in a four-hour in-service in which they learned about science fairs and reviewed the scientific method. They also received instruction on how to implement the research project. Each teacher received a packet of materials that included the pretests and posttests, instructions, and letters to send to parents. Teachers of each of the four treatment groups received different instructions on what to tell the children about the science fair project. For example, "the instructors for the competitive groups . . . were told to remind their students twice a week about the fair and the medals available for the two top projects" (p. 11). Although this statement gives a general idea about what the teachers did, for replication purposes, it would be better to quote the instructions that the teachers gave to the students. When an independent variable is being manipulated through instructions, it is important to know the exact versions of the different instructions.

The study report describes the materials used for the science fair, including a science project notebook and the criteria used to judge the projects. The judges were three college students with experience in science teaching. Students had six weeks to complete their projects. Students worked on the projects on their own outside of the school day, and parents were told to encourage but not help the students. Teachers did not use completed projects to calculate student grades, but it is unclear from the report whether students knew this (which could influence a student's decision to participate).

Regarding treatment fidelity, "impromptu observations made during implementation, and student interviews, which took place after administration of the posttests, were used to verify the treatment" (p. 13). The researcher interviewed three to four students from each class about the instructions the teachers gave to the class. Following up with participants after the study is a good method of documenting treatment fidelity. However, the report does not indicate the number of observations made per class and, more important, does not describe the results of treatment verification. Did the teachers in the different treatment groups give the correct instructions to students? The researcher does indicate that one of the groups did not follow directions and so was not considered in the data analyses.

Data-Collection Instruments and Procedures

The data-collection instruments were two previously published surveys. One survey measured the dependent variable of students' interests in science, and the other survey measured students' attitudes toward science. The researcher describes the items on the two surveys and provides reference information and details on the reliability of the instruments (pp. 9–10). The procedure was for each classroom teacher to administer the surveys to the students before giving the science fair instructions (that is, the treatment) and to administer them again after the science fair was over, with fifteen minutes needed to complete each test. Again, it is important to the study that the teachers gave the pretests and posttests as directed, but the report does not verify this.

Data Analysis and Results

The report gives a detailed presentation on the **descriptive statistics** that were calculated (pp. 15–18). The **means** and standard deviations for scores on the pretest, posttest, and science project are reported for the students in each treatment group. **Frequency distributions** of the pretest and posttest scores are presented in graphs for each treatment group. An extensive display such as this gives the reader an overview of the findings, but descriptive statistics cannot lead to conclusions about treatment effects. In this study, the researcher describes the increases and decreases in scores that occurred but is careful not to base conclusions on the descriptive statistics.

An interesting result of the study was that only five students participated in the voluntary-competitive group, and no students participated in the voluntary-noncompetitive group. As a result, the researcher was unable to analyze whether type of participation in a science fair influences students' interests in and attitudes toward science. But on the basis of this, the researcher suggests, "if students are to benefit at all from science fairs they must be mandatory" (p. 21).

The data for the two remaining treatment groups (mandatory-competitive and mandatory-noncompetitive group) were analyzed through an ANCOVA. (As explained for the Blachman et al. study, ANCOVA controls for the influence of the pretest on the posttest, so that results on the posttest are due to the treatment and not due to preexisting differences.) Only the pretests and posttests for children who completed a science project were analyzed.

Missing data (sample attrition) included one pretest and ten posttests. This is important information, but the researcher does not report in which groups the missing data and resulting participant loss occurred (although in the discussion at the end of the report, it is mentioned that participant loss was evenly distributed among the treatment groups). The results of the ANCOVA demonstrated no significant differences in attitudes toward science of students who participated in either a competitive or noncompetitive science fair. However, students in the noncompetitive science fair had significantly higher interests in science than those in the competitive group (pp. 18–21).

Rival Explanations

In the discussion of the results, the researcher refers back to her research hypotheses, which helps connect the findings to the purpose of the study. She describes how the results relate to findings of prior research studies (pp. 21–22).

The researcher discusses several possible threats to validity (pp. 22–24). She acknowledges that because students were not randomly assigned to the treatment groups, they might have differed in initial characteristics. This is a concern in all quasi-experimental studies. As mentioned previously, one method of addressing the threat of selection bias is to match the groups on characteristics that might influence the dependent variable. Another acknowledged threat to validity was the differences among the teachers in their approach to science teaching. The instruction of the teachers differed in their enthusiasm for science and in their use of inquiry-oriented activities (which was the focus of the science fair). History effects such as these often occur in studies where the treatment is occurring over several weeks or months. In order to understand the results of such a study, the researcher needs to carefully document differences among the treatment groups. Although this researcher mentions the differences, she does not indicate in which groups the differences occurred. Practice effects (that is, from pretest to posttest) were addressed by the use of the ANCOVA statistical procedure that adjusted for pretest scores. A threat to validity not addressed is the possibility of treatment diffusion. Each of the four treatments occurred in each of the two schools. It is likely that students in the different treatment groups (that is, classes) talked to each other about their science fairs and this influenced the decision of those in the voluntary group to participate.

Scientific Characteristics

Blenis provides links with prior research through a review of past research related to science fairs and students' attitudes toward science. She notes the lack of an experimental study on science fairs and therefore the contribution that this study makes to education knowledge. The report lacks discussion of theory especially in the area of rewards and motivation, where there is extensive prior theoretical work. The potential for generalization of the findings from this study is not high because of possible threats to validity from selection bias, history effects, treatment diffusion, and lack of treatment fidelity. Replication is hampered by the lack of details on the treatment (that is, the exact instructions teachers gave to the students). Effect sizes are not reported, so practical significance is not addressed. However, the researcher does discuss how the findings relate to the implementation of science fairs in elementary schools; for example, the need to make science fairs mandatory to have students participate. It is unclear whether the report has been peer reviewed. The source of the report is **ERIC**, the Educational Resources Information Center. ERIC includes many types of reports, many of which are not peer reviewed. For example, one type of ERIC report is a conference presentation. Some conferences accept presentations only after peer review and reviewers' recommendation for acceptance. However, the quality of conference reviews varies greatly, and generally conference paper reviews are not as stringent as the reviews conducted by most journals.

Summary

The education research studies evaluated in this chapter are examples of experimental research designs. The study by Blachman et al. (2004) is an example of a well-executed true experimental design or RCT. The research design is appropriate to the research question. The participants were randomly assigned to the groups so that preexisting differences did not influence the results. The treatment was carefully defined and treatment fidelity was documented. The data were collected using published, reliable instruments. Data analyses were appropriate for the repeated measures in the study, and no claims were made that could not be supported by the findings. The study was peer reviewed and the potential for replication and generalization is high. One concern is the additional aspect of the tutoring treatment that involved neuroimaging and the possible motivational effects of this on the participants. The practical significance of the findings is questionable with respect to the issue of cost.

The study by Blenis (2000) study is an example of a quasi-experimental research design with flaws. The research design is appropriate to the research question but the students were not randomly assigned to the treatment groups (the classes). This lack of random assignment creates selection bias in quasi-experimental studies. Selection bias can be addressed to some degree by matching the treatment groups on characteristics related to the dependent variable. In addition, the preexisting characteristics of participants in the different treatment groups should be carefully described and considered in interpreting the findings related to the treatment. The treatment in this study was based on different teacher instructions to the students, and these were not clearly stated in the report. Treatment fidelity was neither systematically documented nor reported. Published, reliable instruments were used to collect the data. The data were carefully described, and data analyses were appropriate for the repeated measures in the study. The researcher acknowledged a threat to validity due to history effects but did not mention the possible threat of treatment diffusion. The researcher tempers her claims about the findings by calling attention to possible rival explanations. Due to the lack of detail on treatment implementation, the potential for replication and generalization of the findings is low, and there is no indication that the study has been peer reviewed.

Of the two reviewed studies, that by Blachman et al. (2004) is better research primarily because of its systematic selection of participants and implementation of treatment. However, the study was probably very costly to conduct. The Blenis (2000) study illustrates the challenges that individual education researchers face when they have limited funds and want to study applied research questions in schools where random assignment of students to treatments is not feasible. Nonetheless, threats to validity in quasi-experimental studies can be addressed through careful attention to treatment fidelity and efforts to match treatment groups and to document preexisting differences between the groups. In some cases, such differences also can be addressed through **statistical control**.

Chapter 8

Evaluating Descriptive Research Studies

CHAPTER SEVEN DEMONSTRATES the criteria for evaluating **experimental research** studies, and this chapter demonstrates the criteria for evaluating the other major type of research—**descriptive research** studies. It is probably a safe assumption that in education, there are many more descriptive studies than experimental studies. Descriptive studies have the potential to provide important information on what, why, and how things are happening in schools. Unfortunately, many descriptive studies are experimental "wannabes." The researchers of these studies use descriptive methods but they want to make claims about what works. This chapter shows what to look for in a descriptive study to avoid accepting causal claims. It also considers the design features that characterize good descriptive studies.

The two examples that follow are synopses of descriptive studies reported in the education research literature. As in Chapter Seven, each study is summarized and then analyzed by using specific details from the study. Interested readers can obtain the reports and read them in their entirety. The reference information for the reports is available in the References section. (Tips on reading research reports are provided in Appendix A.)

Evaluation of a Comparative-Correlational Descriptive Research Study

All descriptive studies have the same obvious purpose—to describe. As explained in Chapter Three, descriptive studies differ primarily in their complexity and in how the data are collected and analyzed. The study in the first example is a **comparative descriptive** study. It describes and compares data from two groups of participants—teachers and principals—and it also compares different types of teachers. The study is also a **correlational**

descriptive study. It measures the statistical associations between and among several **dependent variables.**

Comparative Descriptive Study: Listening to the Experts: A Report on the 2004 South Carolina Teacher Working Conditions

> The purposes of this study by Hirsch (2004) were to describe teacher working conditions in the state of South Carolina, demonstrate the relationships of these conditions to teacher retention and student achievement, and make recommendations to the state, districts, and schools on how to improve teacher working conditions. Data were collected through an online teacher **survey** that asked teachers about working conditions related to time, empowerment, facilities and resources, leadership, professional development, and induction and mentoring. A separate online survey asked administrators their perceptions of teacher working conditions. Student achievement and teacher retention data were obtained from databases provided by the state. Over 15,000 South Carolina teachers completed the survey, with representation from all the school districts and 90 percent of the schools. The data were analyzed with **descriptive statistics** and **multiple regression analyses.** The primary findings were (1) teacher working conditions predict student achievement, (2) teacher working conditions influence teacher retention, (3) teachers' perceptions of their working conditions reflect reality, (4) teachers and principals have similar perceptions of teacher working conditions, (5) teachers with different experience and background have similar perceptions of working conditions, (6) working conditions are correlated so that if there are positive perceptions of one area, especially of leadership, there are positive perceptions of all the areas. The report concludes with recommendations, including the need for continued study about teacher working conditions in South Carolina, the need to invest in high-quality leadership, and the need to reduce inequities in the mentoring and induction of new teachers.

Research Question

This type of study is often called a policy study because its main purpose is to inform policy decisions, such as legislation and funding allocations. Reports on policy studies usually are written for broad audiences that include people who are unfamiliar with research and statistical terminology. Although this approach is helpful to many readers, it can make it difficult to "unpack" or analyze the study. For example, the Hirsch study lacks a clear statement of the **research question.** Instead, the research question is implied in the introduction to the report as a directive of the South Carolina Teacher Working Conditions to document and analyze teacher working conditions in the state (pp. 1–2). The research question seems to be, What are the working conditions of South Carolina teachers? However, in explaining how the report is organized, the researcher says, "This report demonstrates that working conditions are critical to increasing student achievement" (p. 4). Thus, another research question is, What is the relationship of teacher working conditions to student achievement? The use of the word "increasing" is troublesome because it suggests that a causal relationship is being investigated.

Research Design

The implied research questions indicate that a descriptive **research design** is needed, including one that can examine associations between the dependent variables of working conditions and student achievement. The method section of the report explains that teachers were surveyed about their perceptions of working conditions, and perceptions of teachers with different experiences and backgrounds were compared (p. 3). Multiple regression techniques were used to connect survey responses to student achievement and teacher retention. Although not specified, this explanation of the method indicates a descriptive research design that is both comparative and correlational. The lack of a clear statement about the research design is typical of reports for policymakers and practitioners. The main challenge for the reader is to determine whether the study is descriptive or experimental. Once that determination is made, the rest of the study can be evaluated based on the research design.

Participants

The participants in the study were 15,202 teachers in South Carolina who completed an online teacher survey (p. 3). This number represents teachers from 90 percent of the schools in South Carolina and all of the school districts. An endnote to the executive summary provides a more specific description: "At least one survey was returned from 990 of the state's 1,100 public schools. Surveys were returned from all school districts. . . ." (p. 43). (Notes and appendices are often sources of important technical information in policy reports.) The overall **response rate** for the state was 28 percent, a relatively low response rate, which the report does not address.

A subsample of the teachers was used for the correlational analyses (pp.4–5). There were 519 schools that had a response rate to the survey of at least 28 percent. Teacher responses for these schools were averaged, resulting in school-level scores for the working conditions survey. The researcher demonstrates that this subsample of 519 schools is similar to the other 581 schools in the state by comparing the two groups on demographic and teacher quality characteristics, such as percentage of students eligible for free and reduced lunch, percentage of highly qualified teachers (presumably as defined by NCLB), teacher retention rate, and average teacher salary. A table lists the descriptive statistics for the two groups of schools, but no **inferential statistics** are reported. Nonetheless, the breakdown on the two groups is important for **generalization** purposes. The table suggests that the subsample of schools used for data analyses and conclusions is similar to the other schools in the state (schools with a response rate of 0 percent to less than 28 percent). This means that the findings from the subsample of schools probably can be generalized to the other schools in the state.

Treatment

The concept of **treatment** is associated more often with experimental than descriptive research. In experimental research, the treatment is manipulated so that some participant groups receive the treatment and some do not, or different groups receive different treatments. In descriptive research, the treatment is not manipulated. The researcher studies the treatment "as is." To identify the treatment in a descriptive research study, ask the following question: What program, policy, or practice is the researcher studying? In this example, the researcher is studying teacher working conditions. Two important characteristics of treatments in descriptive studies are the **operational definition** and the **construct validity** of the treatment. In the example, the researcher discusses these in the context of the survey that is used to collect the data about teacher working conditions.

Data-Collection Instruments and Procedures

In the Hirsch study, the **data-collection instrument** is critical to both defining the treatment and to collecting data about it. The report explains in detail how the Working Conditions Survey was developed (pp. 2–3). The survey is a modification of one that the researcher's organization used to study teacher working conditions in North Carolina. That state had conducted focus groups and research to develop standards for teacher working conditions in the categories of time, empowerment, facilities and resources, leadership, and professional development. This work informed the development of a thirty-nine-question paper survey. The survey was then changed to an online format for a second administration in North Carolina. The online survey had seventy-two questions in the same categories but with additional questions on professional development and on work outside the school day. The report noted that some of these new questions were taken from the National School and Staffing Survey and were therefore "previously asked and validated" (p. 2). However, there is no information on the number of such questions or what is meant by "validated" (that is, validated for what?). The North Carolina survey was used in the current study after modification of questions so they were specific to South Carolina and after the addition of questions concerning teacher induction and mentoring.

To establish the construct validity of the Working Conditions Survey, "a statistical factor analysis was conducted not only to ensure that the survey was well-constructed, but also to create domain averages that included only questions that truly explained the working conditions described" (p. 2). In addition, a stakeholder group that included thirty policymakers, administrators, and teachers were asked what questions best explained the different working condition domains. (The domain here refers to the categories of working conditions, such as time and leadership.) The stakeholder results indicated general agreement with the **factor analysis.** An endnote indicates "questions with a factor load of .3 were included in the domain" (p. 44). A factor loading can range from 0 to 1.00, similar to a correlation, so the relationship of individual questions to the domains might be weak. It would help to know the range of factor loadings. Some were presumably higher than 0.3. The report does not provide the **reliability** or internal consistency of the factor domains, which would indicate how well the survey questions for each domain "hang together." Without this information, it is difficult to judge whether a particular domain average is a good measure of the associated working condition. Regarding procedure, teachers' responses were anonymous. This is important information because **participant reactivity** is likely to influence responses under conditions that are not anonymous.

Data Analysis and Results

Almost the entire report is devoted to results and conclusions (pp. 6–37). This is common in policy reports because researchers assume that the results and their implications are the primary concerns of the audience. However, the minimal attention given to methodology makes the evaluation of the methods challenging.

The chapter in the report titled "In-Depth Analysis of Teacher Working Condition Domains" (pp. 16–34) describes, illustrates, and discusses numerous descriptive and some inferential statistics on teachers' responses to the different domains of working conditions. For example, the domain of time had an average rating of 3.11, which was significantly lower than the averages for the other domains. The researcher concluded, "teachers are not satisfied with the time they receive" (p. 17). This statement is difficult to interpret without knowing the scale on which satisfaction was measured. The introduction to the report describes a scale of 1 to 5 but does not indicate whether a 1 means low or high satisfaction. Only by examining the other domains that have higher averages can it be determined that a 1 is low satisfaction. In light of this, a result of 3.11 would not suggest dissatisfaction but rather a neutral attitude. Another conclusion about time is that "it appears that teachers attribute the time dilemma to teaching load and non-instructional duties" (p. 18). However, only 50 percent of the teachers responded in ways that would support this statement. A final conclusion about the domain of time is "teachers are solving the time dilemma by working on school related activities outside of the school day" (p. 18). This statement is based on the finding that 32 percent of the teachers spend ten hours per week outside the school day on activities such as grading and conferences, as well as on other findings indicating teachers are working beyond the school day. Following the presentations on the time domain, the researcher makes some broad recommendations on addressing working conditions related to time.

The presentation format of conclusions, data summaries, and recommendations is used for each of the domains of working conditions that the study addresses. The data summaries in tables and graphs are helpful in explaining the results, but some lack information on the scale used to answer the survey questions. Another concern is the overgeneralization of the results. For example, "only one percent of South Carolina educators indicate that they receive [the] recommended amount of time for collaboration and development" (p. 17). The results actually refer to South Carolina educators who responded to the survey, and this apparently was only 28 percent of the educators.

The chapter in the report titled "What Has Been Discovered About Teacher Working Conditions" (pp. 6–15) describes the results of the correlation and regression analyses for the 519 schools with a survey response rate of at least 28 percent. Schools that achieved the annual yearly progress (AYP) requirements of NCLB were compared to those that did not meet AYP. Teachers in the AYP schools had significantly higher perceptions of working conditions than teachers in the non-AYP schools in each of the five working condition domains. (Mentoring and induction were not considered in this analysis.) The inferential statistic used to analyze these data was not reported. The report indicates that for the regression analysis, survey results on empowerment and professional development were statistically significant predictors of AYP status. The regression results are available in the appendix to the report (pp. 39–41). In another regression analysis, satisfaction with leadership and time were significant predictors of 2003–2004 teacher retention rates. A table presents **bivariate correlations** between each of sixteen working condition–dependent variables (including the five domains, for example, the domain of time, student–teacher ratio, and so forth) and 2003–2004 teacher retention rate. The chapter gives results of correlations and **ANOVAs** for additional findings, such as teacher versus principal perceptions. Overall, the researcher emphasizes the regression results for student achievement (that is, AYP status) and teacher retention, indicating these as new and important findings. However, the researcher uses causal language to describe the results, which is an error in interpretation (pp. 8, 11, 12). For example, "only by controlling for as many of the multitude of factors that contribute to student learning as possible, was the analysis able to isolate the relationship with teacher working conditions and identify causal connections" (p. 8). Statistical modeling through multiple regression is a sophisticated technique that helps identify and measure relationships among dependent variables. However, it does not identify causal relationships.

Rival Explanations

The purpose of many policy reports is to build a foundation of research on which to make recommendations. Perhaps this is the reason there is more attention given to the outcomes and their implications than to methods and **rival explanations.** The Hirsch report addresses rival explanations but they are not labeled as such. All the data in the study come from responses to a survey. A possible rival explanation is that the survey questions do not measure the construct of teacher working conditions but some other construct (for example, teacher experience). The researcher counters this by discussing the development of the survey, including verification of the construct by stakeholders (pp. 2–3). In addition, he reports that teacher background and experience did not affect teachers' perceptions of working conditions (p. 14). In survey studies, low response rate is a threat to validity similar to **sample attrition.** The question is whether the participants who responded to the survey are in some way different from those who did not respond to the survey. The researcher addresses this **threat to validity** by comparing the subsample of 519 schools used for the regression analyses to the other schools in the state (p. 3). The comparisons show that the two sets of schools were similar in characteristics related to student demographics and teacher quality (although statistical tests verifying the similarities are not reported). Perhaps the rival explanations that are of most concern are those related to data interpretation. For example, the suggestion that the findings demonstrate causal connections cannot be supported by the descriptive research design. In addition, the many references to the results of South Carolina teachers are not completely accurate. The results are actually from the 28 percent of South Carolina teachers who responded to the survey.

Translation of research results into accessible language is a particular challenge in reports for policymakers and practitioners. Overstating the findings is a common occurrence. That is why those who read and use research (for example, policymakers) must be able to judge whether the findings justify the conclusions.

Scientific Characteristics

Links with prior research are given in the introduction to the report and throughout the two chapters that present the results. For example, the researcher describes how the survey results for the working condition of facilities and resources relate to results from national studies of that topic (pp. 21–22). The report does not delve into prior **theory** but it does present a clear rationale for the study. The potential for generalization within the state of South Carolina is probably high given the similarity of the sub-sample of schools to the schools that were not in the study. Whether the results would generalize to other states is an interesting question. There is some suggestion that they would, based on a similar study in North Carolina that the researcher describes (p. 2). Replication in South Carolina is likely given the details provided in the method and the availability of the survey instrument on a Website. Although **effect sizes** are not reported, the practical significance of the regression findings is suggested by the strength of prediction (for example, teacher perceptions of empowerment as a predictor of school AYP status, p. 9). The report does not indicate whether it was **peer reviewed.** The publication is a technical report written and published by an organization concerned with teaching quality. Often peer reviews are mentioned in the acknowledgments of technical reports, but that does not occur in this case.

Evaluation of a Qualitative Descriptive Research Study

The most obvious difference between **quantitative** and **qualitative research** is the nature of the data. In quantitative research, the data are numbers, and in qualitative research the data are narrative descriptions. A less obvious difference is that compared to quantitative research, qualitative research gives more emphasis to context and holism and less to isolation and analysis of the object of study into its parts. Qualitative research studies vary in the degree of this contextual emphasis, with more occurring in **ethnographic** and **phenomenological studies.** The study in the following example takes a middle approach to context that is typical of many qualitative education research studies.

Qualitative Descriptive Study: Partners in Professionalism: Creating a Quality Field Experience for Preservice Teachers

The purpose of this study by Grisham, Laguardia, & Brink (2000) was to investigate the quality of the field experience component of a university–school partnership. The partnership had established a professional development school (PDS) arrangement in which five preservice elementary teachers completed their student teaching at one elementary school. PDS activities at the school included teacher study groups on literacy, university classes on literacy methods for student teachers that were also open to the school's teachers, and PDS steering committee meetings that involved teachers, student teachers, the principal, and university professors. The data sources for the one-year study were student teacher **interviews,** classroom **observations,** student teacher and university supervisor journals, and student teachers' project reports. The results indicated unanimous satisfaction by the student teachers with the field experience. Data from the multiple sources were **triangulated** to identify eight factors associated with the quality of the field experience: (1) a year-long field experience in one school, (2) the clustering of several student teachers in one building, (3) the delivery of onsite literacy methods classes, (4) the establishment of teacher study groups and collaborative **action research** projects, (5) the enhanced involvement of university supervisors, (6) the establishment of an active steering committee, (7) the opportunity for student teachers to have a second field experience at a different grade level in the same school, and (8) the enhanced status of student teachers through collaboration with their cooperating teachers. The context of collaboration in the school was important "in establishing and supporting a community of practice in which student teachers flourished" (p. 27).

Research Question

The report provides clear statements of the research questions: "(1) What does it mean for a preservice teacher to have a 'quality' field service experience? (2) What is a quality field experience within a professional development school? (3) Can the teacher/supervisor relationship be expanded to include all the participants in a community of inquiry? (4) What structures can be changed to felicitate the change in the relationship?" (pp. 29–30).

Research Design

The research questions indicate that this is a descriptive research study, and the researchers also clearly state this. "Our research is both descriptive . . . and qualitative" (p. 31). They explain their roles as that of "participant observers." In other words, they were both researchers of the PDS project and also participants in the project. The nature or intensity of their participation is not clear. The biographic information at the end of the report describes the three researchers as university professors of teacher education. In addition, one is the coordinator of the PDS, and a second is the director of the larger school–university partnership program of which the PDS is one project. The third researcher presumably is the person from the university assigned to supervise the student teachers at the PDS. The report refers to the "university researcher," the "university supervisor," the "university professor," the "university participants," but the exact roles of these persons in the PDS project and in the research are not clear.

Participants

The participants in the study were five female student teachers who volunteered to be placed in the PDS for one year and agreed to be subjects in a research study (p. 30). They were all graduate students in a fifteen-month, full-time program that culminated in a master's in teaching degree and in grades K–8 teaching certification. The five participants were informed that participation in the project would involve "substantially more work than the normal program" (p. 30). The report describes the student teaching assignments of each of the five participants, including the characteristics of their cooperating teachers. For example, "Dan was a charismatic teacher who was very popular with the parents" (p. 30). The characteristics of the student teachers also are described. "Laurie was an energetic and gifted student, extremely articulate. . ." (p. 30). However, the details in the descriptions of the student teachers are not systematic across the participants. For example, age was given for only one of the participants. Another concern is the absence of the source for this information (for instance, on what basis or in whose view is Dan "charismatic"?). The researchers were also participants in the study, but as noted previously, clear information on their roles was lacking.

Treatment

As mentioned in the evaluation of the Hirsch (2004) study, in a descriptive study the researcher does not manipulate the treatment but rather studies the treatment in its current state or in some cases in its past state (for example, an **ex post facto research study**). In this study, the treatment is a student teacher field experience. The report provides the operational definition of the field experience through a description of the university program and the PDS (pp. 28–29). The field experience involved one full day and two half days of working with a cooperating teacher in an elementary classroom, which was the normal student teaching experience in the university program. The PDS added the elements of placement in the same school for the entire year, onsite university classes in literacy methods, a required action research project on literacy, and the clustering of five student teachers in one school. An additional attribute of the PDS field experience was the greater presence of the university supervisor than in the normal program, due in part to the clustering of the student teachers but also to the supervisor's involvement in teacher study groups at the school (and in the research conducted for this study).

Data-Collection Instruments and Procedures

Data were collected from multiple sources. There were three formal interviews of each student teacher, one each in November, March, and June. Researchers used a formal **interview protocol,** which was neither described nor included in the report. The researchers interviewed five additional, randomly selected student teachers who were in non-PDS schools. The stated purpose of these additional interviews was for "comparison and triangulation" (p. 31). (The results of the five interviews are alluded to in the report, but specific details are not given.)

The researchers conducted "systematic observations" (p. 31) of the student teachers and recorded these via field notes or videotapes. The report does not indicate the number of observations or what made the observations systematic (for example, the selection of a specific type of lesson for observation or the use of a common **observation protocol**). Other data sources were the action research projects conducted by the student teachers and the cooperating teachers and audiotapes of the PDS steering committee meetings. In qualitative studies, the use of recording equipment lends credibility to the data.

Data Analysis and Results

In qualitative research, the methods of data analysis are particularly important because the results emerge from the researcher's interpretations and are therefore less public than the results of quantitative analyses. The analyses in this study required researchers to first read and re-read the interview data. The researchers "highlighted specific areas of interest" and "consulted each other and other university faculty over these data" (p. 32). The report does not indicate the roles of these other university faculty in the PDS, so their contribution to the data analysis cannot be evaluated. The researchers triangulated data from multiple sources to confirm their initial assertions (p. 32). For example, an assertion about the benefits of clustering student teachers in one school was confirmed by journals, interviews, and observations. The researchers also used triangulation within a data source to confirm an assertion (for example, confirmation of a finding across the different interviews).

The researchers "actively searched the data for **disconfirming evidence**" (p. 32) for their assertions. They also shared the findings with the "informants" in the study—the student teachers, the cooperating teachers, and the principal. This technique is referred to as **member checking** and is a way to verify the accuracy of how the data are represented. For example, a researcher might ask an interviewee to comment on whether the themes identified in the interview data are an accurate reflection of what the interviewee said.

In presenting the results, Grisham et al. (2000) report, "Overall satisfaction with the field experience was unanimous. Exit interviews were both exuberant and positive" (p. 32). They then make eight assertions about the quality of the field experience in the PDS based on evidence in the data. Each assertion is accompanied with references to the data source and, in some cases, examples that support the assertion. For example, for the assertion that the yearlong nature of the student teaching experience was a factor related to its quality, the researchers state that "students felt very much part of the school" (p. 33), and they quote one of the student teachers to support this assertion. For the assertion that clustering of the student teachers in one building was beneficial, the researchers cite the exit interviews as a data source and refer to statements from four of the student teachers. For some of the other assertions, the data are less specific. For example, "journal entries and interviews indicate that supervision was a major element in the satisfaction of student teachers" (p. 35), but there are no quotations to support this statement. The researchers state, "data indicate that one of the most useful functions of the Steering Committee was communication," and this "contributed to the sense of ownership and responsibility that the school faculty felt toward the student teachers" (p. 35). The data for the basis of this assertion are not described.

The lack of details on the data and data analyses in this and other qualitative studies can contribute to a perception that qualitative studies lack rigor. In reality, qualitative studies can be as or more rigorous than quantitative studies. The challenge in qualitative research is to report both the use of systematic data analyses (for example, triangulation) and examples of the data that were analyzed (for example, quotations). In quantitative studies, researchers support their assertions with descriptive and inferential statistics. For example, statements such as "treatment A worked better than treatment B" and "teachers in school A were more satisfied than teachers in school B" are accompanied by means, standard deviations, graphs, ANOVAs, and so on. Without data, claims in quantitative studies cannot be validated, and the same is true for qualitative studies. In an article addressing this issue, Anfara, Brown, and Mangione (2002) describe the importance of making the data in qualitative studies public, and they give suggestions on how to do this.

Rival Explanations

One of the main rival explanations in qualitative studies is that the data do not support the conclusions. In this study, the researchers' data analysis methods help address this threat, including triangulation, member checking, and a search for disconfirming evidence. They also compare multiple sources of data to reach conclusions. However, as discussed, some of their conclusions are not accompanied by evidence. Also, the data collection instruments are not fully described. For example, interviews with student teachers was one of the main sources of data in the study, but the report does not describe the interview protocol or indicate how it was developed or administered. The study does not address participant reactivity as a threat to validity. The researchers were participant observers in the study, and one of the researchers was the university supervisor for the student teachers. If she was responsible for assigning grades for the field experience, then it is possible that responses in the interviews were influenced by the student teachers' desire for good grades. The researchers avoided any references to causal claims, as is appropriate in a descriptive study. They explained how their findings answer their research questions about the characteristics of a quality field experience.

Scientific Characteristics

Grisham et al. (2000) link their study and the results to prior research on school–university partnerships and PDSs (pp. 27–28, 37–38). However, whether the findings can be replicated is questionable. The same results might not occur if the researchers are not also participants in the treatment (that is, the PDS). The potential for generalization is admittedly low. "We do not claim that our findings will generalize to other populations. However, within the qualitative research paradigm the data we collected and analyzed are both compelling and robust for our context" (p. 38). In addition to the context, the characteristics of the participants limit the generalization of the results. The participants were older female graduate students who could participate full time in a yearlong program and who agreed to do the additional work that was required for the research project. The study was published in a journal so the article was peer reviewed, but the nature of the peer review is unknown. To obtain this information it is necessary to consult the journal in which the report was published. The Website for the journal *Action in Teacher Education* reveals that manuscripts are reviewed by members of the Professional Journal Committee of the Association of Teacher Educators, which publishes the journal.

Summary

The education research studies evaluated in this chapter are examples of descriptive research designs. The Hirsch (2004) study is a comparative correlational study in which the purpose was to describe teacher working conditions and their influence on student achievement and teacher retention, and also to make policy recommendations on the basis of the findings. The data-collection instrument was a survey that the report describes in detail. Construct validity of the treatment was established (that is, teacher working conditions), but the reliability of the survey in measuring the treatment was not reported. The report describes the statistical results in detail, although some interferential statistics are not indicated. A problem in the study is the interpretation that findings from the correlational analyses suggest causal relationships. A descriptive research design cannot support causal conclusions. Another concern is the description of the results as applying to all teachers in the state when the response rate was only 28 percent. Overall the study provides important information and recommendations about teacher working conditions in one state.

The Grisham et al. (2000) is an example of a descriptive research study that is typical of many qualitative studies in its design. The participants were purposely chosen to inform the research questions about the quality of a student teaching experience. The researchers collected data from multiple sources in a yearlong study. They used accepted qualitative data analysis methods to support the validity of their interpretations. The main problems with the study are the failure to describe some of the data-collection instruments, provide evidence for some of the conclusions, and describe the roles of the researchers as participant observers. The researchers do not make causal claims, and they admit the limited potential of their findings for generalization, but the study did describe a specific type of teacher education field experience, which was its purpose.

Based on the reports of the two descriptive studies evaluated in this chapter, both studies were well-designed and implemented. The problems in the quantitative study concern the interpretation of the data. When this occurs, those who understand research methods can better evaluate whether an interpretation is correct compared to readers who are less informed. The problems in the qualitative study concern the lack of details on the method and the data. Based on their data analysis methods, it is likely that researchers had the evidence to support their conclusions, but making the data public in qualitative studies can eliminate doubts about the validity of the conclusions.

Chapter 9
Evaluating Literature Reviews

THERE ARE DIFFERENT types of **literature reviews** in education research (Shanahan, 2000). In the introduction of a report on a research study, the author describes how the study relates to prior research on the topic and might refer to that description as a literature review. The purpose is to provide a context for the study. A **research synthesis** is a literature review that systematically summarizes past **empirical research** or **evaluation studies,** or both, on a specific topic. The purpose of a research synthesis is to generate conclusions about a particular topic based on the body of prior research related to the topic. It is important to know the purpose of a literature review, that is, to describe prior research as context for a study or to synthesize prior research to generate new understanding about a topic. This chapter concerns research syntheses.

Unpacking or analyzing a research synthesis involves asking five questions:

1. What is the **research question**?

2. How comprehensive and systematic was the search for past research literature?

3. What were the criteria for including and excluding research studies?

4. How were the results of past research studies coded, analyzed, and summarized?

5. What is the **validity** of the conclusions?

Answering these questions requires an analysis of the research synthesis using the following steps.

Step 1: Identifying the Research Question

In a research synthesis, the researcher poses a question that the synthesis will address. For example: What is the influence of tutoring on student achievement in reading? **Operational definitions** of the terms in the research question influence the scope of the prior research that will be examined. For example, tutoring could be defined as one-on-one instruction of a student by an adult, a peer, or both. Students could be elementary, secondary, or both. Finally, student achievement could be defined as test scores, grades, or both.

Broader definitions are likely to provide more information related to the research question than are narrower definitions. As a result, conclusions will be more trustworthy with broader definitions. For example, tutoring might have different influences on elementary students compared to secondary students. Failure to include studies on both types of students might lead to erroneous conclusions about the overall effect of tutoring on student achievement.

Step 2: Determining Whether the Search for Past Research Was Comprehensive and Systematic

The methods used to search for past research studies are critical to a research synthesis. A comprehensive literature search requires an examination of all potential sources of research literature on a topic. A systematic literature search requires the consistent use of terms in searching for research studies in databases such as **ERIC.** For example, searching for both "tutoring" and "peer-tutoring" in one database and searching only for "tutoring" in another database would not be a systematic literature search and would overlook potentially informative studies.

Step 3: Examining the Criteria for Including and Excluding Research Studies

Most reviewers employ criteria for selecting studies for the synthesis from among the studies produced by the literature search. These criteria and the rationale for their use need to be clearly specified. One common reason to include or exclude studies is their relevance to the research question. For example, for a research question that concerns student achievement in reading, studies that measure only mathematics achievement would be excluded. Another reason to exclude a study is the type of method used to conduct the study. Depending on the research question, some methods would not provide trustworthy results for inclusion. For example, a reviewer might decide to include studies on the effectiveness of tutoring only if they used a **comparison group** of students who did not receive tutoring. Another criterion concerns whether studies have been published in journals or books. Although published studies are more likely to have undergone peer review, journals tend not to publish studies that report negative or no effects of an **intervention.** Consequently, a reviewer who examines only published studies risks making erroneous conclusions about intervention effectiveness.

Inclusion and exclusion criteria should be established prior to the literature search and should be applied consistently to all the studies that the search produces. Otherwise, there could be reviewer bias in selecting studies that have particular results. In addition, the reviewer should describe the number and characteristics of excluded studies.

Step 4: Evaluating the Method Used to Code, Analyze, and Summarize the Results of Past Research Studies

There are different methods for conducting research syntheses. **Narrative review** is a qualitative method that involves summarizing the results of studies through narrative description. Sometimes narrative reviews report the number of positive and negative findings among the studies. **Meta-analysis** is a quantitative method that involves summarizing the results based on their **means** and **standard deviations** (Cooper, 1998). The result of a meta-analysis is an average **effect size,** which indicates the overall impact of the intervention being studied. Meta-analyses use standardized procedures, and syntheses results can be **replicated.** Narrative reviews are less systematic than meta-analyses, and they depend more on reviewer judgment, which makes the syntheses results difficult to replicate. Meta-analyses, however, tend to combine studies together into categories (for example, all tutoring studies of elementary students) so that differences in study details (for instance, the nature of the tutoring) are obscured. In addition, meta-analysis is useful only with **quantitative research** studies.

Before studies can be synthesized, they need to be coded for their various characteristics, such as the **research design** that the studies employed, the nature of the interventions or programs that the studies concerned, and the demographic characteristics of the study participants (for example, student grade level). It is important for the validity of synthesis results that coding is consistent across the different studies. For this reason, when a single researcher codes the studies, a second researcher should double-check the coding. When multiple researchers each code different studies, they should be trained in coding procedures and the reliability (consistency across coders) should be assessed.

Step 5: Judging the Validity of the Conclusions

The validity of conclusions from a research synthesis depends on

- A comprehensive and systematic literature search
- The consistent application of inclusion criteria that are backed by a rationale for their use
- A method of data analysis that is systematic and appropriate to the research question and the type of studies being synthesized
- Reviewer interpretation of the results

The interpretation of synthesis results depends on the judgment of the reviewer who conducted the synthesis. Reviewers should judge results based on the synthesis method and the nature of the studies reviewed. The conclusions should reflect any limitations to the synthesis. For example, the conclusions of a synthesis that examines only published **qualitative research** studies of an intervention can be made only in reference to that body of studies. A synthesis of other types of studies might reach different conclusions. Similarly, reviewers should consider the research quality of the studies in the synthesis when drawing conclusions. If the individual research studies in the synthesis are not valid, then a conclusion based on a synthesis of these studies is unlikely to be valid.

Example of a Research Synthesis

The following is the executive summary of a research synthesis that my colleagues and I at Mid-continent Research for Education and Learning conducted (Lauer, Akiba, Wilkerson, Apthorp, Snow, & Martin-Glenn, 2003). The summary is followed by an analysis of the synthesis report.

> *Research Synthesis: The Effectiveness of Out-of-School-Time Strategies in Assisting Low-Achieving Students in Reading and Mathematics: A Research Synthesis*
>
> The No Child Left Behind (NCLB) Act of 2001 requires states to ensure that all students achieve proficiency in reading and mathematics. States must provide supplementary education services to

low-income students in Title I schools that do not achieve adequate yearly progress toward this goal. Because the instruction for supplementary services must occur outside the regular school day, there is interest among educators in the effectiveness of out-of-school-time (OST) strategies for improving student achievement. Thus, the current synthesis addresses the following research problem: Based on rigorous research and evaluation studies, what is the effectiveness of OST strategies in assisting low-achieving or at-risk students in reading and mathematics?

OST programs vary greatly in their goals and characteristics, and the research on OST has been equally varied. Although some prior reviews of research on after-school programs and summer schools have been conducted, none has systematically examined outcomes in relationship to methodological rigor and content area. To address this need, the current synthesis reviews only studies that used comparison or control groups to reach conclusions, and it provides separate analyses of OST strategies for student achievement in reading and in mathematics.

An exhaustive literature search was conducted to identify both published and unpublished research and evaluation studies conducted after 1984 that addressed the effectiveness of a program, practice, or strategy delivered outside the regular school day for low-achieving or at-risk K–12 students. The search resulted in 1,808 citations, from which 371 reports were obtained. Among the criteria for synthesis inclusion were that studies had to measure student achievement in reading and/or mathematics and employ control/comparison groups. Fifty-three studies met the inclusion criteria, 47 with reading outcomes and 33 with mathematics outcomes. Of the 53 studies, 27 addressed outcomes in both subject areas.

Researchers used a coding instrument to describe the following for each study: characteristics of the OST strategy and the students it addressed, research design and methods, data analyses and findings, and research quality. The latter concerned the degree to which studies had four types of validity: construct, internal, external, and statistical. To produce consistency among judgments, researchers trained on the use of the coding instrument and used procedures for double-checking their coding results.

The studies were analyzed through meta-analyses and supplemented by narrative descriptions. Results were further analyzed for the influence of moderators on the effectiveness of OST strategies. Program moderators included time frame (after school or summer school), grade level of the students, focus of the OST activities (academic or academic plus social), duration of the OST program, and grouping of students (large or small groups or one-on-one tutoring). Study moderators included research quality (high, medium, or low), publication type (conference paper, dissertation, or peer-reviewed journal article), and score type (gain score or posttest score).

The synthesis resulted in statistically significant positive effects of OST on both reading and mathematics student achievement. The overall effect sizes ranged from .06 to .13 for reading and from .09 to .17 for mathematics, depending on the statistical model used for meta-analysis. Though numerically small, these results are important because they are based on strategies to supplement the regular school day and to prevent learning loss. Positive findings for supplementary programs that address the needs of low-achieving or at-risk students are therefore encouraging. Together, the results for reading and mathematics suggest that OST programs can significantly increase the achievement of these students by an average of one-tenth of a standard deviation compared to those students who do not participate in OST programs. (pp. 1–2)

The authors then summarize how different variables moderated the effectiveness of the OST strategy. For example, whether the time frame was after school or summer school did not significantly influence achievement. However, program duration was a **statistically significant** moderator of effect sizes for both reading and mathematics outcomes. Effect sizes for OST programs that were 45 hours or less in duration were not statistically significant. The authors report that the largest positive effect occurred with the use of one-on-one tutoring in reading.

In addition to the analyses of study outcomes, the syntheses of reading and mathematics studies described some common features among the studies in each content area. In reading, these were the links between student attendance and student achievement, the importance of staff quality, the development of academic and social skills, the implementation of a well-defined reading curriculum, and the prevention of learning loss. Common features highlighted in the mathematics studies were additional time for remediation, the use of tutoring, the use of counseling and mentoring, and the combination of recreation with mathematics instruction.

Overall, the meta-analytic and narrative results led to the following conclusions and implications for practice and policy related to OST and its evaluation:

- OST strategies can have positive effects on the achievement of low-achieving or at-risk students in reading and mathematics.
- The time frames for delivering OST programs (i.e., after school or summer school) do not influence the effectiveness of OST strategies.
- Students in early elementary grades are more likely than older elementary and middle school students to benefit from OST strategies for improving reading, while there are indications that the opposite is true for mathematics.
- OST strategies need not focus solely on academic activities to have positive effects on student achievement.
- Administrators of OST programs should monitor program implementation and student learning in order to determine the appropriate investment of time for specific OST strategies and activities.
- OST strategies that provide one-on-one tutoring for low-achieving or at-risk students have strong positive effects on student achievement in reading.
- Research syntheses of OST programs should examine both published and unpublished research and evaluation reports.
- Future research and evaluation studies should document the characteristics of OST strategies and their implementation. (pp. 3–4)

The Research Question

The research question is, What is the effectiveness of out-of-school-time (OST) strategies in assisting low-achieving students in reading and mathematics (p. 6)? My colleagues and I (hereafter referred to as "the authors") define an OST strategy as a program, practice, or intervention delivered outside the regular school day. The authors explain that the most common OST strategies are after-school programs and summer schools (p. 8). They define low-achieving students as those in grades K–12 who are identified as low-performing based on an academic assessment or who are at risk for being low performing based on previously identified risk factors, such as high poverty (p. 15). Achievement was defined in quantitative studies as academic achievement in reading, mathematics, or both based on classroom assessments, standardized tests, or grades in subject areas. In qualitative studies, achievement was defined as student learning in reading, mathematics, or both based on qualitative documentation.

Comprehensive and Systematic Search for Past Research

The researchers describe in detail their search for research studies related to the research questions, including the keywords and terms they used to search the ERIC database, the *PsychInfo* database, and *Dissertation Abstracts* (pp. 13–14). They read **abstracts** of the 1,746 citations obtained from the searches, examined them for relevance to the synthesis based on their inclusion criteria, and obtained the full reports for 309 studies. They ordered sixty-two additional research studies from reference citations on Websites and in research articles and evaluation reports, resulting in a total 371 reports that they read from a total of 1,808 citations.

Criteria for Including and Excluding Research Studies

The report lists the criteria for including studies and explains the rationale for the criteria (pp. 15–17). For example, a research or evaluation study had to be published or reported in or after 1985 because that date was the approximate start of the standards movement in the United States. Quantitative studies had to include a **control-comparison group** and use **experimental** or **quasi-experimental research** designs due to the authors' "emphasis on rigor" (p. 15). They included both published and unpublished studies because they wanted to avoid a bias in favor of finding positive results. "It is particularly important to examine unpublished studies on OST programs because many of them are evaluations that are disseminated as technical reports for organizations rather than published in peer-reviewed journals" (p. 15).

The authors identified fifty-three studies that met their criteria for inclusion in the research synthesis, and they excluded 250 studies. They describe the main reasons for excluding a study as the lack of a control or a comparison group, the failure of the study to target low-achieving or at-risk students, and the lack of student achievement data in reading or mathematics.

Analysis and Summary of Results of Past Research Studies

The report describes how the studies were coded and analyzed (pp. 17–22, Appendixes A and B). The researchers participated in coder training and double-checked their coding decisions. The studies that had sufficient quantitative information were analyzed via meta-analyses, and the rest of the studies were synthesized through narrative review. Graphs illustrate the effect sizes of the studies that measured student achievement in reading and mathematics achievement (pp. 37, 60), and tables show the influences of program and study characteristics on the overall average effect sizes obtained from the meta-analyses (pp. 38–41, 62–64). Results for studies that were analyzed through narrative review were described as "mostly positive," "mostly negative," or "even" with respect to the influence of OST strategies on student achievement (pp. 43, 65).

The results of the narrative review were mixed, so the researchers drew conclusions based primarily on the results of the meta-analyses. Meta-analysis produces a quantitative summary of varying results from different studies, which makes an interpretation error less likely than analysis based on narrative review. The researchers considered the research quality of the studies in the synthesis by including only those studies with control or comparison groups and by examining the influence of research quality on the effect sizes of the studies. (Each study was coded for research quality, but quality rating had minor influence on the effect sizes of the studies.)

Conclusions from a synthesis are valid only for the studies that are included in the synthesis. As the researchers of this synthesis indicate, they excluded 250 studies for not having comparison groups or sufficient documentation on student achievement. If these studies could have been included, the results might have been different. The researchers also point out that many of the included studies failed to describe details of the OST programs (for example, student attendance, teacher characteristics), which made it difficult for them to give recommendations about specific OST practices that might improve student achievement (p. 76).

Although this synthesis report was not published in a peer-reviewed journal, the acknowledgments in the report indicate that three external reviewers provided input.

The report by Lauer et al. (2003) provides an example of what to look for when evaluating a synthesis. Other examples of systematic research syntheses include a meta-analysis of the effects of comprehensive school reform models on student achievement (Borman, Hewes, Overman, & Brown, 2003) and a narrative review of the relationship of teacher characteristics to student achievement gains (Wayne & Youngs, 2003). Both were published in the *Review of Educational Research,* a respected peer-reviewed research journal, and both are models of good research syntheses.

Chapter 10

Assessing the Relevance of Education Research

AFTER READING REPORTS on education research studies and making a judgment about whether the results and conclusions can be trusted, practitioners and policymakers need to decide whether and how the research should be used to influence education practice or policy. Local and state factors, including the cost of implementation, are obvious influences on practice and policy decisions. In addition, the quality, coherence, applicability, and educational significance of the research should be considered. This chapter examines each of these factors and concludes with a tool for assessing research utility.

Research Quality

The quality of education research is influenced by whether the research is

- *Valid.* High-quality education research studies have conclusions that can be trusted. **Research designs** match **research questions,** and data collection and **data analyses** follow accepted technical standards.

- *Connected to prior research.* High-quality education research studies build on prior research studies and conclusions. Research reports indicate how the studies contribute to the current knowledge base on education.

- *Ethical.* High-quality education research studies follow established rules of **research ethics.** Procedures are used to avoid **researcher bias.**

- *Peer reviewed.* High-quality education research studies are reviewed by other education researchers before the findings and conclusions are widely communicated.

Research Coherence

The coherence of education research is influenced by whether the research findings

- Are based on a **theory** or conceptual framework. A theory provides the rationale for the research design and guides the interpretation of the results. Because theories propose explanations for observations, theory-driven research gives practitioners and policymakers the reasons behind particular findings on a policy issue.

- Have been **replicated.** Findings that have been replicated in several studies provide a stronger basis for making practice or policy changes than those from only one study.

- Are part of a body of research. A body of research on an education program or policy provides conclusions about an issue or program from different studies in various settings and with various participants. A body of research is more informative than are a few disconnected studies. (For an example of a body of research, see the literature review on summer school by Cooper, Charlton, Valentine, and Muhlenbruck [2000].)

Research Applicability

An important factor that influences whether an education research study should be used to guide practice or policy is the degree to which the findings of the study apply to the situation of interest to the practitioner or policymaker. Researchers call this the **external validity** of the research.

Setting

One consideration that influences applicability is the comparability of the setting of the research study and the setting of interest. For example, research on a teacher professional development program in urban school districts might not be applicable to a state in which rural schools are the norm, particularly if teacher collaboration between schools is an important feature of the program. The distances between rural schools could make teacher collaboration very difficult.

Participants

A second consideration is the comparability of the participants. There is a lack of research, for example, on curricula and instruction for students from ethnic minorities. Participants in most education research studies are white, which calls into question whether the results apply to participants from ethnic minority backgrounds.

Yet another example is that many research studies on the effectiveness of education programs and practices do not **disaggregate** the results for low-achieving or at-risk students. A program that facilitates learning for average students might not help struggling learners. The No Child Left Behind Act requires that states disaggregate state test results for subgroups of students. This requirement is resulting in increased research on what can help low-achieving students meet state standards.

Program or Treatment

A third consideration is the comparability of the program or **treatment.** Unless the treatment or program described in the research study is similar to that of the situation of interest, there can be no expectation that the results of the treatment in the situation of interest will be similar to those observed in the research study. For example, if the research study involved giving students laptop computers to take home as part of their language arts curriculum, using the same curriculum but without the laptop computers might not have the same effect.

Education practitioners can help policymakers determine whether a research study or group of studies is applicable to a particular local context. Practitioner knowledge, also referred to as **professional wisdom,** is an important source of information about the realities of classrooms and schools and the influences of local circumstances. If research settings do not match local contexts (for example, research on urban schools applied to a rural state), policymakers must determine the likelihood that the same results will be obtained in their schools. Practitioners can be of great assistance in this situation.

Educational Significance

An important question for those who use research is, What is the educational significance of these findings? In other words, what difference will it make to education if a practice or policy is changed or adopted based on research results? Without knowing the educational significance of a research finding, it is difficult, if not impossible, to estimate the costs and benefits of changes in practice or policy.

One indicator of educational significance in a research study is the **effect size** of a program or practice. (Researchers refer to effect size as the **practical significance** of a result, in contrast to its **statistical significance.**) There are some limitations to effect sizes. Their calculation requires **quantitative data.** In addition, effect sizes that are reported in individual research studies indicate the educational significance of a program or practice only for the specific participants and settings in that study. In other words, effect sizes might not apply to the local context in which the program or practice is implemented. For example, an effect size for a program designed for elementary students might be different if the program is implemented with middle school students. As discussed in Chapter Nine, a **meta-analysis** reports an average effect size across several studies of an education program or practice. For this reason, a meta-analysis provides more information for determining educational significance than a single research study.

A Balancing Act

In the end, it is a matter of balancing all the criteria of usefulness in a way that reflects the local circumstances involved in a particular practice or policy decision. First, it is necessary to determine whether the research is **empirical** and the researcher's conclusions are valid. Next, the practitioner or policymaker must decide how much weight to give to the other criteria of research usefulness. The costs of educational decisions and potentially harmful effects are factors that should always be considered in addition to the information provided by the research. When there is little or no useful research on an education topic related to an education decision, and a change is needed or mandated, ways should be found to fund the necessary research. In the long run, a decision that is informed by research might be far less costly than one that is uninformed.

Research Utility Assessment Guide

The Research Utility Assessment Guide (Exhibit 10.1) is designed to help assess the utility or relevance of a particular research study. The guide considers study characteristics related to the relevance and utility of a study. It is a heuristic tool for examining a research study, but it is not intended to provide a precise measure. In addition, practice and policy changes should be made based on a large body of evidence and not on the basis of a single study.

EXHIBIT 10.1

Research Utility Assessment Guide

Questions to ask   Rating +/−/?

Empirical evidence:

   1. Is the research based on observations as opposed to advocacy / opinions only?

If no (−), STOP! Do not use this study for changing practice or policy. Find empirical research related to the topic

Validity: Is the research study valid with regard to:

   2. Match of the research question and the research design?

   3. Participants and their selection?

   4. Treatment definition and implementation?

   5. Data-collection instruments and procedures?

   6. Data analyses?

   7. Ruling out rival explanations?

If there are four or five minuses, PAUSE! Consider finding other empirical research related to the topic. If there is no validity (all minuses), STOP! Do not use this study for changing practice or policy.

Applicability: Is the research study similar to the situation of interest in its . . .

   8. Setting?

   9. Participants?

  10. Program or treatment?

If there is no applicability (all minuses), PAUSE! Consider looking for empirical research that has greater applicability (also called "external validity").

Practical Significance: Does the study have practical significance as indicated by . . .

11. Positive effect size?

12. Cost considerations?

Coherence:

13. Is the study based on a theory or conceptual framework?

14. Do the study results have support from prior research?

Peer Review:

15. Has the study been peer reviewed?

Bias:

16. Does the study avoid researcher or evaluator bias?

Final Score:

Total number of pluses

Total number of minuses

Total number of question marks

Assessment Guide Scoring Directions

Answer the questions in numerical order. For each numbered question, if the answer is yes, score a plus (+) in the right-hand column. If the answer is no, score a minus (–) in the right-hand column. If uncertain about how to answer the question, indicate a question mark (?) in the right-hand column.

All pluses—This study is highly useful for making practice and policy decisions.

Majority pluses—This study is useful for making practice and policy decisions. Examine the characteristics that received the fewest pluses. Consider how the lack of those characteristics could affect the study's usefulness.

Equal pluses and minuses—This study has limited usefulness for making practice and policy decisions. Examine the characteristics that received minuses. Consider how the lack of those characteristics could affect the study's usefulness.

Majority minuses—This study is not useful for making policy decisions. Look for other empirical research related to the topic before using this study.

Majority question marks—If the question marks are due to a lack of information provided in the study, consider contacting the researcher for that information. If the question marks are due to a lack of understanding about the study characteristics, an inability to judge their presence in the study, or both, consult this primer, other resources on education research, or seek the help of an education researcher.

Example of How to Assess Research Utility

The following example illustrates how an actual education research study might be evaluated using the Research Assessment Utility Guide.

Quasi-experimental Study: An After-school Intervention Program for Educationally Disadvantaged Young Children

The purpose of this research study by Bergin, Hudson, Chryst, and Resetar (1992) was to investigate the effects of an after-school program on the literacy achievement of at-risk kindergarten students. Twelve African American kindergarten students who lived in subsidized housing participated for sixteen months in an after-school program that included culturally relevant reading activities. Their results on standardized reading tests were compared to those of a similar group of kindergarten students who were not participating in the after-school program. The researchers reported that the students in the treatment group had statistically higher achievement scores on tests of reading and reading readiness than the students in the **control group.** In addition, the treatment but not the control students were above the national norm in some areas of the tests. The researchers reported **qualitative data** from treatment **observations** and **interviews** of teachers, parents, and students that suggested additional benefits of the program, including students' increased enthusiasm for learning.

Questions to Ask

1. Is the research based on observations as opposed to advocacy or opinions only?

   Yes (+)

   The study is based on observations of the literacy achievement of kindergarten students.

2. Is the study valid with regard to a match of the research question and the research design?

   Yes (+)

   The research question is causal: Does an after-school program improve the achievement of kindergarten students? The study uses a **quasi-experimental** research design. A treatment group was compared to a control group, but participants were not **randomly assigned** to the two groups.

3. Is the study valid with regard to participants and their selection?

   No (–)

   Students volunteered for the after-school program. Treatment and control students were equally distributed between two kindergarten classes in the same school and were from the same subsidized housing complex. However, there were no **data** to support the equivalence of the treatment and control groups in literacy achievement prior to implementation of the after-school program.

4. Is the study valid with regard to treatment definition and implementation?

   Yes (+)

   The report gives a detailed description that **operationally defines** the treatment (that is, the after-school program) and its implementation. The curriculum, the teachers, the schedule, and the setting are all described. In addition, the report gives an example of a teacher–student interaction based on observations of the after-school sessions.

5. Is the study valid with regard to **data-collection instruments** and **procedures**?

   No (−)

   The report describes an achievement test and a readiness test and indicates that both are **standardized tests.** However, there is no reference information provided for the tests and there is no information regarding **test validity** or **reliability.** Interviews and observations were conducted, but the report does not describe the **interview protocol** or **observation protocol** used to collect these data.

6. Is the study valid with regard to data analyses?

   Yes (+)

   The analyses are appropriate for the data from the two literacy tests. The **inferential statistics** are reported, and there are graphs of the **descriptive statistics.** The researchers also collected qualitative data from observations and interviews, but they do not report how they analyzed those data, so validity of the data is questionable. However, the quantitative data constitute the primary source of evidence in the study.

7. Is the study valid with regard to ruling out **rival explanations**?

   No (−)

   The main rival explanation for the results is **selection bias.** There is no evidence to show that the treatment and control groups were equivalent in literacy skills prior to the implementation of the after-school program. In addition, the students in the treatment group were volunteers. Their motivation for performing on the tests might have been greater than that of the control students who did not participate in the after-school program. The researchers acknowledge these rival explanations but provide no evidence to rule them out.

8. Is the research study similar to the situation of interest in its setting?

   Yes (+)

   Assuming that the situation of interest is after-school programs for at-risk students, the setting would be similar, as the treatment occurs in a community building in a low-income neighborhood.

9. Is the research study similar to the situation of interest in its participants?

   No (+)

   The characteristics of the participants make the study findings difficult to **generalize** to other situations. There are too few participants, they are volunteers, and they represent one ethnic minority and one grade level.

10. Is the research study similar to the situation of interest in its program or treatment?

Yes (+)

The treatment is similar to other after-school programs. However, this program also had some unique characteristics. For example, the teacher aides were undergraduates from a university teacher-preparation program, and the head teacher was supported by a university research assistantship.

11. Does the study have practical significance as indicated by positive effect sizes?

Yes (+)

The researchers report positive effect sizes of $d = 0.83$ for auditory skills, $d = 0.51$ for visual skills, and $d = 0.83$ for prereading skills (pp. 210–211). (See the Statistics Tutorial in Appendix C for an explanation of how to interpret effect sizes.)

12. Does the study have practical significance as indicated by cost considerations?

No (−)

The report does not provide the actual costs, but it does describe the funding sources. The program was staffed by volunteers and had support from the university through the undergraduates, who were teacher aides, and through a research assistantship for the head teacher. There were small grants from the public schools and a local business. It is difficult to determine whether this program would be cost-effective if there were no volunteers or grants.

13. Is the study based on a theory or conceptual framework?

Yes (+)

The researchers describe theory and prior research that support the design of the after-school program. They cite the importance of culturally relevant instruction for minority children and the importance of offering choices so that children have perceptions of control over their environment.

14. Do the study results have support from prior research?

No (−)

The researchers cite only two studies on the effects of increased instructional time for low-achieving students, and they do not relate their results to the larger body of research on out-of-school time (for example, studies of summer schools).

15. Has the study been peer reviewed?

    Yes (+)

    The study was published in a journal, and so peer review is probable.

16. Does the study avoid researcher or evaluator bias?

    Cannot be determined (?)

    The report describes the after-school program as "a research and demonstration project initiated by university faculty members in collaboration with public school personnel" (p. 205). University undergraduates helped staff the program, but the report gives no details about who collected the reading achievement data or how the data were collected. However, the researchers report corroborating data from teachers' grades on report cards. The treatment students received significantly higher reading grades and higher ratings for reading efforts from their teachers than the students in the control group. There were no statistically significant group differences in math grades, and there were also no group differences on the quantitative components of the achievement and readiness tests. (The after-school program emphasized literacy.) This pattern of results suggests that researcher bias did not influence the findings, but without more documentation of the **research method,** bias cannot be ruled out.

Scoring Summary

On the Research Assessment Utility Guide, the Bergin et al. (1992) study was scored with ten pluses, five minuses, and one question mark. According to the scoring directions, this study is useful for making practice and policy decisions. The characteristic that received the fewest pluses was validity (three pluses and three minuses), which indicates the possibility that the conclusions cannot be trusted. Before investing in a large-scale implementation of the program, it would be worthwhile to replicate the study.

Appendix A

Tips on Reading Research Reports

Sources of Education Research

A **primary source** is a report of an original research study. A primary source usually provides enough details to **replicate** the research study. Primary sources are written by the researcher(s) or evaluator(s) who conducted the study. The main formats of primary sources are journal articles, technical reports from research institutions or education organizations, and reports on presentations at conferences.

A **secondary source** is a description and summary of one or more prior research studies. Secondary sources usually do not include enough details to replicate the original studies being described. Examples of secondary sources are **literature reviews** and books. Although newspaper articles also can be secondary sources, they often do not have enough information to help readers form a solid judgment about the research. Essays by education experts can be secondary sources of education research, but essays can be overly biased toward the views of the writer.

Caution: Secondary sources have the potential to distort original research findings and can lead to conclusions that are based more on interpretation and opinion than on fact. Many debates about education topics arise because secondary sources draw conclusions that the original research does not warrant. When in doubt, always consult the original research study.

Use primary sources when it is important to know the details of a study and its results. Use secondary sources to obtain an overview of the research on a particular topic and reference information for original research studies (McMillan, 2000). For example, to research the topic of professional development schools for teacher preparation, start with a secondary source such as the *Handbook of Research on Teacher Education* (Sikula, Buttery and Guyton, 1996). This book has chapters written by education researchers on various topics related to teacher education. Then consult the primary sources cited in the chapter on professional development schools.

Reading Reports on Education Research

Reports on education research tend to follow similar formats. There are some differences, however, depending on whether the report concerns a **research study,** an **evaluation study,** or a literature review.

Reading Research Studies

Most reports that are primary sources on education research studies follow a common organization.

1. **Abstract** or executive summary. Gives a brief but comprehensive summary of the research report, including the **research problem,** the **research method,** the results, and conclusions. Always read the abstract or executive summary first because it is designed to organize the reader's thoughts about the content of the report.

2. Introduction. Describes the research problem, the background of the problem, related prior research, and the purpose and rationale for the study. It also gives a brief overview of the research method used. The introduction usually concludes with specific **research questions** and sometimes with the **research hypothesis.**

Caution: In reports on research studies, the author describes in the introduction how the study relates to prior research on the topic. Sometimes the author refers to this description as a literature review. Because, however, the purpose is to provide a context for the study and not to produce new conclusions based on past research, this description is not a literature review as defined in this primer as a stand-alone synthesis.

3. Method. Provides information on how the study was conducted, ideally with enough details so the study can be repeated. Typically, the method section describes the following (not necessarily in this order):

- **Research design** or plan for gathering the data
- Characteristics of the study participants and how the researcher selected the **sample** of participants
- **Procedure** or implementation steps used by the researcher
- Materials (for example, a reading curriculum) and **data-collection instruments** used in the study

4. Results, findings. Describes the results or findings of the research study. The format of the results section depends on the type of research questions

the study addressed and the type of research design the study used. The results section usually begins with a description of the **data-analysis plan,** although sometimes this is explained in the method section. The results section ends with a summary of the results or findings. As might be expected, the results section for **quantitative research** study reports many numbers and **statistics.** The results section for a **qualitative research** study primarily reports **narrative descriptions** of the findings. If the results section seems overwhelming, read the summary of the results first. The summary provides the most important information about the findings without getting bogged down with technical details. When there is no summary at the end of the results section, look for one at the beginning of the discussion section.

5. Discussion, conclusions. Summarizes the results and relates them to the research questions and hypotheses described in the introduction. In the discussion, the researcher provides the rationale for why the results support or do not support a particular conclusion. The researcher also discusses **rival explanations** and limitations of the study. The discussion section often ends with suggestions for future research that might clarify or extend the study findings.

Caution: An author's conclusions often go beyond what is really justified by the research results or findings and may involve the author's own subjective interpretations. The conclusions of a research study thus generally should be carefully scrutinized to see whether they truly follow from the findings.

6. References. Lists a bibliographic reference for every citation that occurs in the report. The references section is a good source for finding other research reports related to the topic of the study.

Reading Reports on Evaluation Studies

Reports on evaluation studies are less rigid in structure than research reports because the format of evaluation reports depends on the audience. Evaluation reports published in academic journals are more likely to resemble research reports than those that are unpublished or published in other formats, such as technical reports for school districts. Most reports that are primary sources on evaluation studies follow a common organization (Weiss, 1998).

1. Executive summary. Gives a comprehensive summary of the report, including a program description, **evaluation questions,** method, findings, and recommendations. Always read the executive summary first because it provides an overview and enough details to understand the evaluation outcomes.

2. Program description. Describes the education program that is being evaluated, including program goals, activities, participants, and staff. Also

provides context such as the history of the program and its relationship to the community.

3. Evaluation description. Describes the evaluation questions and the **evaluation design.** Also briefly describes the methods used to collect data, but technical details, such as data-collection instruments, are discussed in an appendix to the evaluation report.

4. Results, findings. Presents the main findings of the evaluation study. Each finding is accompanied by supporting evidence from statistics or narrative descriptions. More detailed results are described in an appendix to the evaluation report.

5. Conclusions. Presents the evaluator's interpretation of the findings, including limitations of the evaluation study.

Caution: An author's conclusions often go beyond what is really justified by the evaluation results or findings and may involve the author's own subjective interpretations. The conclusions of an evaluation study thus generally should be carefully scrutinized to see whether they truly follow from the findings.

6. Recommendations. Suggests recommendations about the program based on evaluation results. (Whether or not recommendations are included in an evaluation report depends on the goals of the evaluation study.)

Caution: The recommendations an author gives necessarily involve the author's own interpretations and values and thus always go somewhat beyond the study's results and findings. Recommendations should not be considered matters of fact.

7. Appendix. Provides additional information and technical details about the program being evaluated, the evaluation method, the data-collection instruments, and the results.

Reading Reports on Literature Reviews (or Research Syntheses)

Literature reviews are secondary sources on research. Literature reviews describe and summarize past reports on research, evaluation studies, or both. The purpose of a literature review is to provide new conclusions about the body of prior research related to a specific topic, such as the effects of summer school on student achievement. (Another term for a literature review is **research synthesis.**) Literature reviews vary in method and scope, so the structure of literature reviews varies as well. Most literature reviews, however, have certain standard components.

1. Abstract or executive summary. Summarizes the purpose, method, findings, and conclusions of the literature review.

Caution: Abstracts and executive summaries of literature reviews sometimes are misleading. Results from a literature review depend on how the reviewer analyzed reports on prior research. To better understand and evaluate the results and conclusions of a literature review, always read the sections in the review that explain the process used to select and analyze research studies.

2. Introduction. Describes the topic and purpose of the literature review. Sometimes a research question is posed. For example, "Based on past research, does summer school improve student achievement?"

3. Background. Provides background information related to the topic. The reviewer usually discusses the history behind the topic and why the topic is important in the current education context. The reviewer also indicates how the terms in the topic are defined for purposes of the review. For example, a review of research on teacher mentoring should define what constitutes teacher mentoring.

4. Method. Describes the method used to search for, select, and analyze past research studies. The method is a critical component of a literature review because the results and conclusions depend on the scope of the search for past studies, the criteria used to include or exclude studies, and the method used to analyze the studies.

There are two general methods of analysis used for literature review: **narrative review** and **meta-analysis.** In a narrative review (also called a qualitative review), the reviewer interprets the studies by describing, comparing, and contrasting the studies and their results. In a meta-analysis (also called a quantitative review), the reviewer uses statistics, primarily **effect sizes,** to summarize the results of different studies. (See the literature review on summer school by Cooper, Charlton, Valentine, and Muhlenbruck [2000] for an example that uses both narrative review and meta-analysis.)

5. Results. Provides the results of the literature review. The results section often includes a table that lists the citations for the reviewed studies and briefly describes the methods and findings of each study. In a narrative review, the author usually organizes results based on a particular aspect of the topic. For example, in a narrative review of research on summer school, the reviewer might discuss the results from studies of summer mathematics programs and of summer reading programs separately. In a meta-analysis, the reviewer also might organize results by subtopic and indicate effect sizes for the subtopics.

6. Conclusions. Summarizes the results of the review and presents conclusions. The author usually discusses limitations of the review based on either the method used to review the studies or the characteristics of the studies themselves. The **validity** of the conclusions of a literature review depends on whether the reviewed studies are of adequate research quality. Look for whether reviewed studies were examined for their research quality.

Appendix B

Glossary of Education Research Terms

Abstract: A brief, comprehensive summary of a research report that includes the research problem, a description of the participants, and an overview of the method, results, and conclusions.

Action research: A type of research in which educators examine their own practices and evaluate strategies to improve practice and education outcomes. Action research conducted by groups of individuals, such as school staffs, is called collaborative action research. Most action research studies use descriptive research designs.

Aggregated data: Data for which individual scores on a measure have been combined into a single group summary score.

> *Example:* In education research, it is common to aggregate individual student scores on an achievement test into a mean score for each school. Researchers then use the aggregate school achievement score for data analyses. Aggregating data reduces the sample size and obscures differences among individual scores.

Analysis of variance (ANOVA): A statistical technique used to test for statistically significant differences between two or more groups of observations. An ANOVA produces F, an inferential test statistic.

Attitude scale: A questionnaire that gathers information about participants' attitudes or beliefs concerning a particular topic based on the degree of intensity that they indicate in their responses.

Bivariate correlation: A statistical correlation between two variables.

Blind data collection: A method in which those who are collecting the data for a study are unaware of the treatment groups to which participants have been assigned.

Case study: A data-collection method in which a single person, entity, or phenomenon is studied in depth over a sustained period and through a variety of data.

> *Example:* A researcher conducts a yearlong case study of a school district that was awarded a grant to improve teacher quality. The researcher documents the processes used to implement the grant, interviews teachers and administrators, observes staff development, and measures student achievement before and after the grant was awarded.

Central tendency: A score in a set of scores or a frequency distribution that is typical or representative of all the scores. Measures of central tendency are the mean, median, and mode.

Coding: In qualitative research, the process used to reduce information into categories or themes for data analysis and interpretation.

Coefficient of determination: For bivariate correlations, the coefficient of determination is defined as r^2, which is interpreted as the proportion of variation in the scores that is explained by the association or relationship between the variables. *Note:* Correlations indicate statistical, not causal, relationships.

> *Example:* A researcher finds a correlation of $r = 0.60$ between years of teaching experience and student achievement. The coefficient of determination of $r^2 = 0.36$ means that 36 percent of the variation in achievement scores can be explained by the relationship between the two variables. (Conversely, 64 percent of the variation in achievement scores cannot be explained by the relationship.)

Collaborative action research: Research in which educators jointly examine their practices and evaluate strategies to improve practice and education outcomes. Most action research studies use descriptive research designs.

Comparative descriptive research design: A research design in which data are collected to describe and compare two or more groups of participants or entities.

> *Example:* A researcher identifies high-poverty schools in the state that have either high or low student achievement. The researcher describes the alignment or match between each school's curriculum and state standards and compares the high- versus the low-achieving schools to determine whether the degree of alignment is different.

Comparison groups: The groups of participants who are being compared in a study, either based on different group characteristics or on having different treatments.

Confidence interval: A range of values that indicates the confidence or probability of observing a particular score or value in a population, usually expressed as standard deviation units above and below the mean. The wider the interval, the greater the confidence or probability that a particular value will be observed.

> *Example:* Based on a random sample of fourth grade reading scores, a researcher calculates the following 90 percent confidence interval for the mean of the population of fourth grade reading scores: 67 ± 3.2. This indicates there is a 90 percent probability that the mean reading score of the population is between 63.8 and 70.2.

Construct validity: The degree to which variables in a research study are considered by the education and research communities as acceptable representations of the constructs that the study concerns.

> *Example:* One-on-one instruction is a valid representation of the construct of tutoring, while whole-class instruction would not be considered valid. Student scores on a standardized mathematics test are a valid representation of the construct of student achievement, while student scores on a survey about attitudes toward school would not be considered a valid representation.

Content validity: The degree to which the items on a measuring instrument (for example, test or questionnaire) adequately cover the content that the instrument is designed to measure.

Control: The strategy used in scientific research to regulate the effects of variables in a study that are not intended to influence the results or conclusions.

> *Example:* A researcher conducts a study of two teacher preparation courses on how to teach mathematics. The researcher controls for differences among preservice students by randomly assigning the students to one of the two courses. The researcher controls for differences among course instructors by having a single instructor teach both courses.

Control group: The group of participants in an experiment who do not receive the treatment that is being studied.

Convenience sample: A sample of participants selected for a research study based on their availability.

> *Example:* A teacher educator conducts a research study of the preservice students enrolled in the traditional and alternative teacher-preparation programs at the institution where the teacher educator is a faculty member. The sample is one of convenience because the preservice students are selected for the study based on their availability to participate.

Correlation coefficient: A number that indicates the strength and direction of the statistical association between two or more variables. Correlation coefficients vary between –1.00 and +1.00. The higher the numerical value, the stronger the association. A correlation of 0.00 indicates the absence of an association. A positive sign means that as one variable increases, so does the other. A negative sign means that as one variable increases, the other variable decreases.

> *Example:* A correlation coefficient of +0.63 between the number of education courses and teacher test scores means that the more education courses that a teacher candidate completed, the higher the test score. A correlation of –0.63 means that the more education courses that a teacher candidate completed, the lower the test score. Neither correlation coefficient, however, can support the existence of a causal relationship between courses and test scores because correlation is not causation.

Correlational research: A type of research that seeks to establish an association or correlation between two or more variables. The fact that two or more variables are associated does not necessarily mean that one is a cause of the other(s).

Correlational research design: A research design in which data are collected to describe the statistical association between two or more variables.

> *Example, bivariate correlation:* In school district X, a researcher collects data on beginning teachers' scores on the state licensing test (variable 1) and data on the achievement gains of each teacher's students (variable 2). The researcher then uses correlational statistics to measure the association between the two variables.

> *Example, multivariate correlation* (also referred to as multiple regression): In school district X, a researcher collects data on beginning teachers' scores on the state licensing test (variable 1), the number of college courses that each teacher completed in mathematics (variable 2), the amount of time that each teacher spent in school-based field

experiences prior to certification (variable 3), and the achievement gains in mathematics by each teacher's students (dependent variable). The researcher uses multiple regression statistics to measure the association between the three teacher variables and student achievement gains and to estimate student achievement gains based on the contribution of each of the teacher variables to that association.

Covariate: A variable that is correlated with another variable, such that when there is a change in one variable, there is a corresponding change in the other variable. Analysis of covariance is a statistical method that controls for the influence of covariates on the dependent variable in a research study.

> *Example:* A researcher conducts a study on the influence of teacher professional development on principals' ratings of teacher performance. The researcher designates teaching experience as a covariate to statistically control its influences on principal ratings.

Criterion variable: The dependent variable that is being predicted in a regression analysis.

Criterion-referenced test: A test for which a score is interpreted by comparing it to levels of performance established for the test by professionals in the field that the test addresses.

> *Example:* Scores on the Colorado Student Assessment Program are assigned to the following categories based on the proficiency that students demonstrate in relation to state content standards: unsatisfactory, partially proficient, proficient, and advanced.

Cross-sectional research: A data-collection strategy in which data are collected at one point in time from participants who are at different developmental or grade levels. The purpose is to draw conclusions about differences between developmental groups.

> *Example:* A researcher conducts a study of a new standards-based mathematics curriculum to determine whether the curriculum benefits students differently depending on their grade levels. The researcher compares gains in mathematics achievement by second, fourth, and sixth graders after their school adopts the new curriculum.

Data: Factual information gathered as evidence for a research study.

Data-analysis plan: The plan for analyzing data in a research study. In a quantitative research study, the data-analysis plan provides details on statistical procedures. In a qualitative research study, the data-analysis plan provides details on coding procedures.

Data-collection instrument: A tool used to collect data in a research study such as a test, observation protocol, or questionnaire.

Degrees of freedom (df): In statistics, the number of scores in a sample that are free to vary, calculated as sample size minus one ($n - 1$). The degrees of freedom are used in the calculation of inferential statistics.

Dependent variable: The variable that is measured in a study. In an experimental research study, the dependent variable is affected by the independent variable. In a correlational research study, the dependent variable is associated with one or more other variables.

> *Example, experimental research study:* A researcher randomly assigns teachers in a large elementary school to receive one of three types of professional development: (1) a class on instructional strategies, (2) a training program on how to increase student motivation, or (3) a teacher discussion group. The researcher measures the differences in achievement gains among the students of the three teachers. The dependent variable is student achievement gains.

> *Example, correlational research study:* A researcher collects data on beginning teachers' scores on the state licensing test (variable 1) and data on the achievement gains of each teacher's students (variable 2). The researcher then uses the association between the two variables to estimate student achievement gains. The dependent variable is student achievement gains.

Descriptive research: A type of research that has the goal of describing what, how, or why something is happening.

Descriptive statistics: Statistics used to describe, organize, and summarize data.

> *Example:* Commonly used descriptive statistics include the mean, median, and standard deviation.

Disaggregated data: Aggregated or grouped data that have been separated into individual component scores.

> *Example:* The No Child Left Behind Act requires schools to disaggregate student achievement data into the scores obtained by subgroups of students based on race-ethnicity, disability, socioeconomic level, gender, migrant status, and English language proficiency.

Disconfirming evidence: A method used to verify the accuracy of data analyses in qualitative research by searching for evidence that negates the themes and categories that the researcher used to code and analyze the data.

Education research: The systematic gathering of empirical information to answer questions related to education.

Effect size: The degree to which a practice, program, or policy has an effect based on research results, measured in standard deviation units. (Effect size is also referred to as practical significance.) A statistic commonly used to measure effect size is Cohen's *d*, which some social scientists interpret as the following: $d = 0.2$, small; $d = 0.5$ to 0.8, medium; and $d = 0.8$ and higher, large. (In correlational studies, effect size is measured by the coefficient of determination.)

> *Example:* A researcher finds an effect size of $d = 0.5$ for the effect of an after-school tutoring program on reading achievement. (See Figure B.1.) This means (provided that the research study is valid) that the average student who participates in the tutoring program will achieve one-half standard deviation above the average student who does not participate. If the standard deviation is eight points, the effect size translates into four additional points, which might increase a student's ranking on the test.

Empirical information: Information based on something that can be observed. Students' test scores, observations of teachers' classroom instruction, principals' interview responses, and school dropout rates are examples of empirical information in education research.

FIGURE B.1

Effect Size

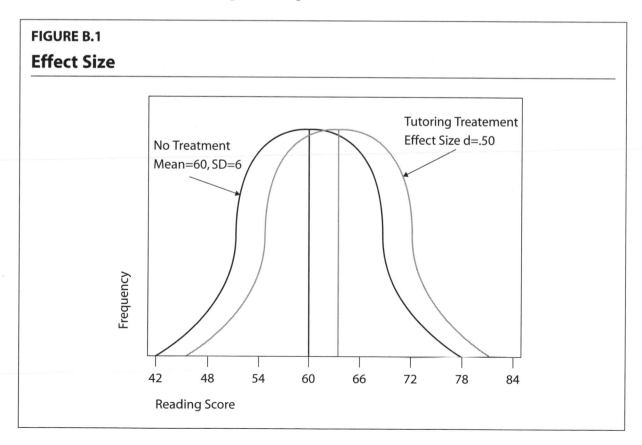

Empirical research: Research that seeks systematic information about something that can be observed in the real world or in the laboratory.

ERIC: The Educational Resources Information Center, a federally funded source for literature on education research, including a searchable online database. See http://www.eric.ed.gov.

Error: Inaccuracies in implementing a research study, including during sampling, treatment delivery, data recording, or data analysis. Errors increase the variability of the data and threaten the validity of research conclusions.

Ethnography: A data-collection method in which information is collected about a group of individuals in their natural setting, primarily through observations.

> *Example:* A researcher uses ethnography to study the challenges that face three beginning teachers at one elementary school. The researcher observes and documents the teachers in their classrooms, on the playground, in the teachers' lounge, at staff meetings, at parent conferences, and in staff development sessions.

Evaluation design: The plan for how data will be collected in an evaluation study. The evaluation design should be appropriate for the evaluation questions that the study addresses.

Evaluation question: The question(s) that an evaluation seeks to answer about a program. Evaluation questions can address program processes, program outcomes, links between the processes and outcomes, and explanations for the outcomes.

Evaluation study: A study designed to judge the utility and effectiveness of an education program. A formative evaluation provides information about improving program implementation. A summative evaluation assesses program outcomes and effectiveness. Some evaluations include both formative and summative information. Evaluation studies use some of the same research designs that research studies employ.

> *Example:* A school district hires an evaluator to conduct a study on the effectiveness of an after-school tutoring program. The evaluator collects data about the student participants, their achievement before and after tutoring, the type and amount of tutoring that occurred, and the characteristics of the tutors. The evaluator also collects achievement data from a comparison group of students who applied too late to receive tutoring. The evaluation results include data about changes in student achievement (summative data), as

well as data about whether the program was implemented as planned and how it might be improved (formative data).

Experimental research: A type of research that has the goal of determining whether something causes an effect.

Experimental (true) research design: A research design in which (1) an independent variable is directly manipulated to measure its effect on a dependent variable and (2) participants are randomly assigned to different groups that receive different amounts of the independent variable. (Also referred to as a randomized controlled trial or a randomized field trial.)

> *Example:* A researcher randomly assigns thirty teacher-preparation candidates to participate in one of three student teaching programs: (1) no student teaching, (2) eight weeks of student teaching, or (3) sixteen weeks of student teaching. (See Figure B.2.) After the candidates graduate, the researcher compares their scores on a performance-based teacher licensing test. The type of student teaching is the independent variable, and performance on the teacher licensing test is the dependent variable. Groups 1 and 2 are the treatment groups because they participate in student teaching. Group 3 is the control group because the participants do not participate in student teaching. Together the three groups make up the comparison groups.

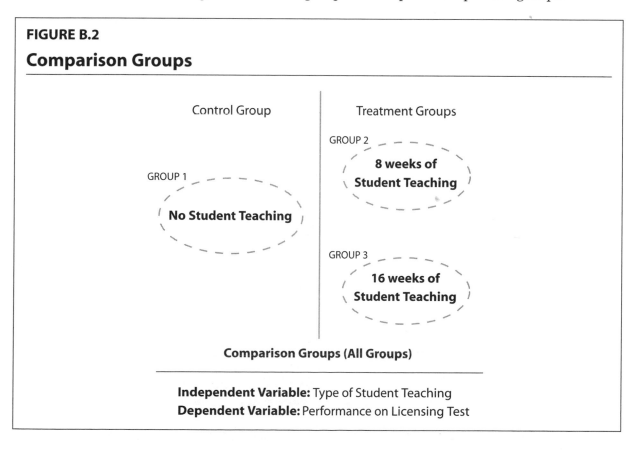

FIGURE B.2

Comparison Groups

Control Group

Treatment Groups

GROUP 1

No Student Teaching

GROUP 2

8 weeks of Student Teaching

GROUP 3

16 weeks of Student Teaching

Comparison Groups (All Groups)

Independent Variable: Type of Student Teaching

Dependent Variable: Performance on Licensing Test

Ex post facto research: Descriptive research that examines the influence of a preexisting independent variable or treatment.

> *Example:* A researcher conducts a study to compare two reading programs. The participants are students in School A, which has been using Reading Program A for three years, and students in neighboring School B, which has been using Reading Program B for three years. This study is ex post facto because the research concerns effects from a preexisting treatment.

External validity: The degree to which results from a study can be generalized to other participants, settings, treatments, and measures.

Extraneous variables: Variables in a research study that are not intended to influence the results or conclusions. Researchers use various methods to control the influence of extraneous variables.

> *Example:* A researcher conducts a study of the effects of two reading curricula on first grade reading achievement. Extraneous variables in this study include students' verbal abilities and teachers' characteristics. The researcher needs to control the influence of these extraneous variables on achievement, possibly by having one teacher instruct both curricula and by randomly assigning students to the curricula.

Factor analysis: A statistical procedure that reduces a set of items on a measuring instrument into a smaller number of dimensions called factors.

> *Example:* A researcher creates a twenty-four-item questionnaire on teachers' classroom practices in language arts. A factor analysis reduces the twenty-four items into three factors. Factor one has eight items related to using drills and worksheets, factor two has six items related to independent reading, and factor three has ten items related to whole-class instruction.

Field test: A trial run of all or some parts of a research study, including the treatment, data-collection procedures, and data-collection instruments. Researchers often test their data-collection procedures and instruments in the field, using the persons and contexts for which the procedures and instruments were designed. Developers often field-test their education programs, materials, and assessments prior to their publication.

Focus group: A group of participants who are interviewed together and encouraged to share their opinions on a particular topic.

Frequency distribution: The frequency of occurrence of scores in a set. Frequency distributions can be represented in graphs or tables. (See Table B.1.)

TABLE B.1

Frequency Table

Mathematics Score	Frequency	Percent	Percentile
50	1	10.0	10.0
51	2	20.0	30.0
52	1	10.0	40.0
53	1	10.0	50.0
55	3	30.0	80.0
58	2	20.0	100.0
Total	10	100.0	

Example: Scores on a mathematics test: 51, 52, 51, 55, 55, 53, 58, 50, 55, 58

Generalization: The replication of research results in different contexts and with different populations.

Goodness-of-fit statistics: Statistics used to evaluate how well a set of scores or results conforms to a predicted frequency distribution or to a hypothesized model.

Grounded theory: A qualitative research method in which the researcher creates a theory from the categories that emerge from an extensive collection of qualitative data.

Hierarchical linear modeling (HLM): A statistical technique used to analyze data from participants who exist within different levels of a hierarchical structure.

> *Example:* Student achievement data reflect influences from the family, classroom, grade, school, district, and state. Through HLM, the influences of these different levels on student achievement can be estimated.

History effect: A threat to the validity of research conclusions due to events that occur in the time between a pretest and a posttest. The longer the time span between a pretest and posttest, the more likely the occurrence of history effects.

> *Example:* A researcher randomly assigns eight elementary schools to participate in Reform Model A and eight elementary schools to participate in Reform Model B. The researcher measures student achievement prior to implementation of the reform models (the pretest). After one school year, the researcher measures student

achievement again (the posttest). Events that occur between the pretest and posttest can influence the results. For example, perhaps a large number of teachers in B schools enroll in graduate school, which improves their teaching.

Hypothesis, null: A statement that an independent variable or treatment will have no effect. Researchers attempt to demonstrate through data that the null hypothesis is false.

Hypothesis, research: A statement about the researcher's expectations concerning the results of a study.

> *Example, nondirectional research hypothesis:* A change in high school class schedules will have an effect on student attendance.

> *Example, directional research hypothesis:* A change in high school class schedules will increase student attendance.

Independent variable: In experimental research, the variable that the researcher varies or manipulates to determine whether it has an effect on the dependent variable.

> *Example:* As part of an experiment, a researcher randomly assigns teachers in a large elementary school to receive one of three types of professional development: (1) a class on instructional strategies, (2) a training program on how to increase student motivation, or (3) a teacher discussion group. The researcher measures the differences in achievement gains among the students of the three teachers. The independent variable is professional development.

Inferential statistics: Statistics used to make inferences about a population based on the scores obtained from a sample. Inferential statistics are based on the mathematics of probability theory. Commonly used inferential statistics include t, F, and Chi Square.

Internal validity: The degree to which the conclusions of a research study are supported by evidence and can be trusted.

Inter-rater reliability: The degree of agreement in the ratings that two or more observers assign to the same behavior or observation.

Intervening variable: An unmeasured variable that is assumed to intervene between a treatment or independent variable and a behavior or dependent variable. Most intervening variables are internal and cannot be observed. Their existence is inferred based on external measures.

> *Example:* Learning is an intervening variable because it cannot be observed but is assumed to occur between instruction and performance based on measures such as tests.

Intervention: A procedure, technique, or strategy that is designed to modify an ongoing process. In research studies, the intervention also is referred to as a treatment. Most interventions in education are designed to modify directly or indirectly the student-learning process.

Interview: A data-collection method in which the researcher asks questions of individuals or groups and records the participants' answers. The interviewer usually asks the questions orally in a face-to-face interaction or over the telephone, but electronic interviews administered through e-mail also are possible.

Interview protocol: The planned questions and accompanying probes asked during an interview. Structured interview protocols ask specific objective questions in a predetermined order. Unstructured interview protocols ask open-ended questions and the order depends on interviewees' answers.

Latent variable: An unobserved variable that is hypothesized to have an influence on a dependent variable. Latent variables can be analyzed through the statistical technique of structural equation modeling (SEM).

> *Example:* A researcher studies the relationship of school environment to student achievement. School environment is a latent variable that reflects the observed variables of parent involvement, orderly school climate, emphasis on student achievement, and use of assessment and monitoring practices. The researcher measures the observed variables through a teacher survey.

Likert scale: A response scale in which participants respond to questionnaire items about their beliefs and attitudes by indicating varying degrees of intensity between two extremes such as like-dislike and agree-disagree.

Literature review: A comprehensive and systematic summary of past empirical research or evaluation studies on a specific topic. (Another term for a literature review is research synthesis.)

Longitudinal research: A data-collection strategy in which data are collected from the same participants at different points in time. The purpose is to draw conclusions about individual change over time.

> *Example:* A researcher studies the mathematics achievement of students who were taught a new standards-based mathematics curriculum when they were in sixth grade. The researcher compares students' performances in mathematics achievement in grades seven, eight, and nine to the performances of another group of students at each of those grade levels who were not taught the new curriculum in sixth grade. The purpose of the research is to determine whether

change in mathematics performance over time is related to the type of sixth grade mathematics curriculum.

Matching: A procedure used to select participants for comparison groups based on participant characteristics that are related to the dependent variable. Matching is frequently used in quasi-experimental studies when random assignment to groups is not feasible.

> *Example:* A researcher assigns fifteen teacher-preparation candidates who have a seminar on Wednesdays to participate in eight weeks of student teaching. The researcher finds a group of fifteen teacher-preparation candidates who have a seminar on a different day and who are similar to the Wednesday group in the number and type of courses completed. The researcher assigns this second group of candidates to participate in sixteen weeks of student teaching.

Mean: In general, the average score in a set of scores or frequency distribution, calculated as the sum of the scores divided by the number of scores.

> *Example:* The mean of the following set of five scores is 11: 9, 10, 10, 12, 14.

Median: The middle score in a set of scores or frequency distribution such that 50 percent of the scores are at or below the median score.

> *Example*: The median of the following set of five scores is 10: 9, 10, 10, 12, 14.

Member checking: A method used to verify the accuracy of data analyses in qualitative research by asking participants to review the findings and comment on the accuracy of the themes and categories that the researcher identified.

Meta-analysis: A comprehensive, systematic, quantitative review of past empirical research studies on a specific topic. Most meta-analyses examine only quantitative studies. Effect-size statistics are calculated to produce an overall conclusion about the various studies on the topic.

> *Example:* A researcher conducts a meta-analysis of computer-assisted instruction in reading. The researcher examines forty studies and calculates an overall effect size of $d = 0.25$, indicating a small positive effect of computer-assisted instruction on reading achievement.

Mixed methods: The use of both quantitative and qualitative data-collection strategies in the same study. By providing more and different types of information related to the same research question, this approach can increase the reliability and applicability of research conclusions.

Mode: The most frequent score in a set of scores or a frequency distribution.

> *Example:* The mode for the following set of five scores is 10: 9, 10, 10, 12, 14.

Mortality: A threat to the validity of research conclusions due to the loss of participants from a study sample (also referred to as sample attrition).

Multiple methods: The use of more than one research method in a single research study, such as an experimental research study that includes descriptive research to verify that a treatment was implemented correctly.

> *Example:* A researcher conducts an eight-week study of the effects of cooperative learning on student achievement. The researcher randomly assigns half of a teacher's students to participate in cooperative learning groups and the other half to participate in small-group instruction. To verify treatment implementation, the researcher conducts systematic observations of both the cooperative learning and the small-group instruction groups. This study uses both experimental and descriptive research methods.

Multiple regression analysis: A statistical technique that determines the linear association between a set of predictor variables and a dependent variable and identifies the combination of predictor variables that best estimates the dependent variable (also referred to as the criterion variable).

> *Example:* In School District X, a researcher collects data on beginning teachers' scores on the state licensing test (predictor 1), the number of college courses in mathematics that each teacher completed (predictor 2), the amount of time spent in school-based field experiences prior to certification (predictor 3), and the achievement gains in mathematics by each teacher's students (criterion variable). The researcher uses multiple regression statistics to measure the association between the three teacher variables and student achievement gains and to estimate student achievement gains based on the contribution of each of the teacher variables to that association.

N (n): The number of scores in a population (*N*) or in a sample (*n*) of scores.

Narrative descriptions: Verbal descriptions of the information obtained from qualitative research such as descriptions of interview results.

Narrative review: A type of literature review in which research studies and their results are interpreted through narrative descriptions and qualitative comparisons.

Normal curve: The bell-shaped curve that results from the graph of a normal frequency distribution.

Normal curve equivalent (NCE) scores: Percentile scores from a normal frequency distribution that have been converted so there is an equal interval between each NCE score.

Normal distribution: A symmetrical frequency distribution in which the scores form a bell-shaped curve and the mean, median, and mode have the same value. (See Figure B.3.)

FIGURE B.3

Normal Distribution

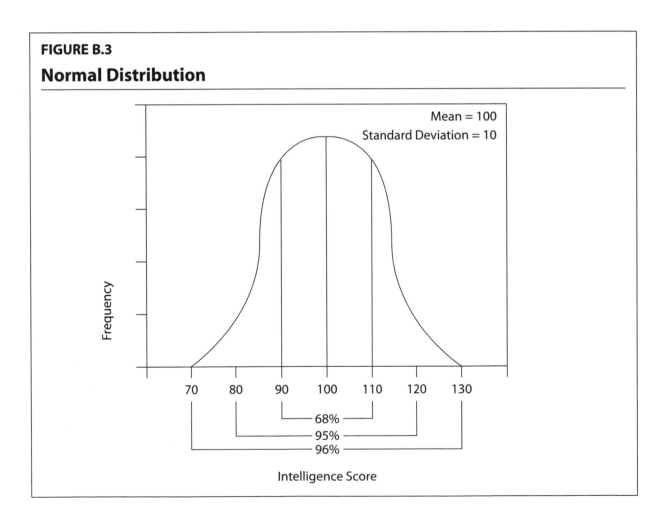

Norm-referenced test: A test for which a score is interpreted by comparing it to the scores of a comparison or norming group of persons who took the test. The similarity of an individual to the persons in the comparison group influences the accuracy of interpretation.

> *Example:* The SAT, which students take to gain admission to institutions of higher education, is a norm-referenced test. A score on the SAT is interpreted with reference to the scores of other students who took the test. Originally, a score of 500 on the SAT was considered average because that was the average score of the comparison or norming group of students.

Observation: The collection of data by documenting the occurrence of events in a setting. Observation is a common method of data collection in qualitative research.

Observation protocol: The plan for conducting observations of an event or behavior, including the frequency and duration of observations, and the definition of what will be observed.

Operational definition: A definition of a variable based on the methods used to measure or produce it.

> *Example:* An operational definition of student proficiency might be a score on an achievement test that is at or above 60 percent correct. An operational definition of an after-school tutoring program might be one-to-one tutoring of children by adults in reading and mathematics for two hours immediately after school, twice a week.

Percent: The proportion of participants who obtain a particular score in a frequency distribution.

> *Example:* In the frequency distribution shown in Table B.2., 20 percent of the participants obtained a mathematics score of 88.

Percentile: The percentage of participants who score at or below a particular score in a frequency distribution (also referred to as percentile rank).

> *Example:* In the frequency distribution shown in Table B.3, 80 percent of the participants obtained a mathematics score of 48 or lower, which means that a score of 48 is at the 80th percentile.

TABLE B.2

Percent

Mathematics Score	Frequency	Percent	Percentile
85	3	30.0	30.0
86	1	10.0	40.0
88	2	20.0	60.0
91	2	20.0	80.0
92	1	10.0	90.0
96	1	10.0	100.0
Total	10	100.0	

TABLE B.3

Percentile

Mathematics Score	Frequency	Percent	Percentile
45	1	10.0	10.0
46	1	10.0	20.0
47	4	40.0	60.0
48	2	20.0	80.0
49	1	10.0	90.0
50	1	10.0	100.0
Total	10	100.0	

Peer reviewed: A research study that has been critiqued by other researchers prior to publication or presentation at a research conference. (The quality of peer review varies among different publications and professional organizations.)

Phenomenological study: A qualitative research method in which the researcher conducts an in-depth and extensive study of participants' experiences of an event or situation from the participants' perspectives.

Pilot test: A trial run of all or some parts of a research study, including the treatment, data-collection procedures, and data-collection instruments. (See also field test.)

Population: All individuals or entities belonging to the group that is being studied.

Example: Examples of populations are all elementary school teachers in the United States, all schools in the Midwest, all fourth grade students in Colorado, and all high school teachers in School District X.

Practical significance: The degree to which a practice, program, or policy has enough of an effect to justify its adoption. Practical significance usually is measured with statistics that calculate effect sizes.

Predictor variable: The variable in a regression analysis used to predict the value of a dependent variable.

Pretest-posttest research: Research in which participants take a pretest that measures the dependent variable prior to the administration of a treatment and a posttest that measures the dependent variable after the treatment is completed. The most valid approach to implementing pretest-posttest research is to randomly assign participants to two or more groups, one of which receives the treatment. The pretest-posttest difference scores are then compared for the groups.

> *Example:* A researcher randomly assigns middle school students to participate in either an inquiry-based science unit or a traditional science unit. The students complete a test on problem solving before and after the unit. Because the problem-solving skills of the students in the inquiry-based group improved more than those of the students in the traditional group, the researcher concludes that inquiry-based units facilitate problem-solving skills.

Primary source: A report on an original research study, usually written by the researcher(s), which includes details about the method and results.

Procedure: The specific steps that are taken to implement a research study.

Professional wisdom: The judgment that individuals acquire through experience, including the ability to incorporate local circumstances into practices and policies.

Proxy: A measure used to approximate the data sought when it is difficult to obtain a more precise measure due to constraints involving data collection or time.

> *Example:* Average passing rate on state licensing tests by teacher candidates is a proxy measure for the quality of teacher-preparation delivered by teacher education institutions.

Purposive sample: A sample of participants selected for a research or evaluation study based on the information that they can provide related to the study.

> *Example:* A researcher conducts case studies of four teacher-preparation programs that received recognition for their effectiveness in preparing teacher candidates. The sample is purposive because the programs were chosen based on their recognition.

Qualitative data: Narrative descriptions or observations.

Qualitative research: Research in which the data are narrative descriptions or observations. In most qualitative research, there is an emphasis on the influence of context.

> *Example:* A researcher observes how teachers deliver instruction related to different reading curricula in two schools. The researcher also interviews the teachers to understand their approaches to the different curricula and how their approaches might be influenced by school characteristics.

Quantitative data: Numbers and measurements.

Quantitative research: Research in which the data are numbers and measurements. In quantitative research, there is an emphasis on control of the variables in the study.

> *Example:* A researcher randomly assigns students to different reading curricula. At the end of the school year, the researcher examines the students' scores on a reading achievement test to determine whether the different curricula had different effects on reading.

Quasi-experimental research design: A research design in which (1) an independent variable is manipulated to measure its effects on a dependent variable and (2) the participants in the comparison groups are not randomly assigned to those groups.

> *Example:* A researcher assigns fifteen teacher-preparation candidates who have a seminar on Wednesdays to participate in eight weeks of student teaching. The researcher assigns fifteen teacher-preparation candidates who have a seminar on Tuesdays to participate in sixteen weeks of student teaching. After the candidates graduate, the researcher compares their scores on a performance-based teacher licensing test. The amount of student teaching is the independent variable, and candidate performance on the teacher licensing test is the dependent variable. The researcher does not randomly assign candidates to the comparison groups. As a result, differences between the groups' performance on the test could be due to the amount of student teaching or due to other characteristics of the teacher candidates. The researcher should demonstrate that the candidates in the two groups do not differ in characteristics that are related to teaching performance.

Random assignment: The assignment of participants to comparison groups via chance procedures so that every participant has the same probability of being selected to a group. (See Figure B.4.)

Random sample: A sample that is randomly drawn from a population so that each member of the population has an equal probability of being chosen for the sample. (See Figure B.5.)

Randomized controlled trial: A "true" experimental research design in which (1) an independent variable is directly manipulated to measure its effect on a dependent variable (that is, the treatment trial) and (2) participants are randomly assigned to different groups that receive different amounts of the independent variable (that is, the treatment). (Also referred to as a randomized field trial.)

Range: The difference between the highest and lowest score in a set of scores or frequency distribution.

> *Example:* The range for the following set of five scores is 5: 9, 10, 10, 12, 14.

Raw score: An original score on a test or other measuring instrument prior to any score transformations.

FIGURE B.4

Random Assignment

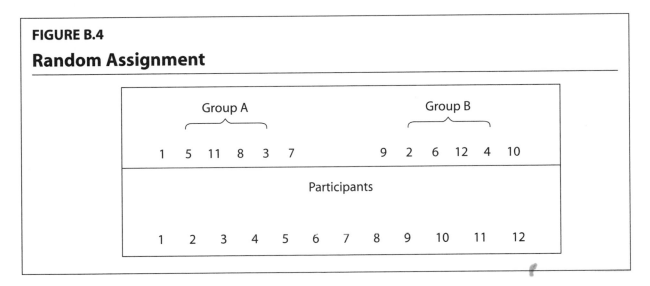

FIGURE B.5

Random Sample

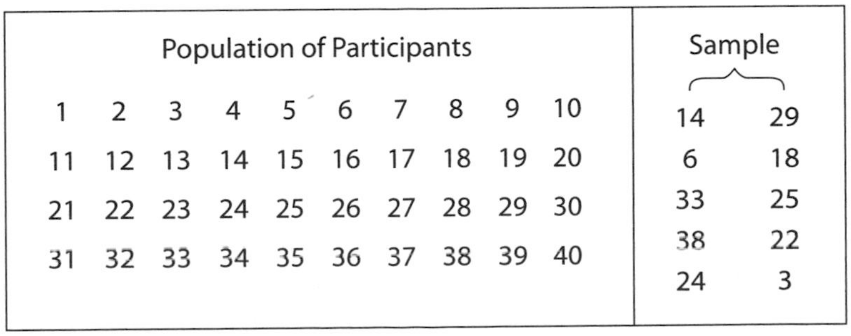

Reactive measure: A measure toward which a participant is likely to react due to interactions with the researcher or the participant's assumption that certain responses are desirable.

Example: Interview questions are reactive measures because interviewees respond to actions by the interviewer (such as a head nod) that indicate approval or disapproval of the interviewees' answers.

Regression analysis: A statistical technique that uses the relationship between two variables, X and Y, to predict the value of X based on observations of Y.

Regression toward the mean: The tendency for extreme scores to move toward the average or mean score when a test or other measure is repeated. Regression effects threaten the validity of research conclusions in studies in which participants are chosen because of their extreme scores on a measure.

Example: Researchers often study schools in which students have extremely low achievement scores. If these students improve their achievement following a treatment or intervention, the improvement could be due to regression effects instead of treatment effects. In such studies, it is important to have comparison schools of students who also have extremely low achievement scores but who do not receive the intervention.

Reliability (of a measuring instrument): The extent to which a measuring instrument produces consistent results when it is administered again under similar conditions.

Example: A reading test is reliable if students obtain similar scores when they take alternate but equivalent forms of the test within a short time span.

Reliability coefficient: A correlation coefficient that indicates the degree of relationship between two sets of scores that result from persons taking a test again under similar conditions. Reliability coefficients also indicate the degree of relationship among a set of items on a questionnaire or test.

Example: A test-retest reliability coefficient of 0.91 for a mathematics achievement test indicates that the test produces consistent results. A reliability coefficient of 0.51 for the internal consistency of an attitude questionnaire indicates that the questionnaire items have only a moderate relationship to one another.

Repeated measures: A research study in which participants are measured two more times on the same dependent variable.

> *Example:* A researcher conducts a study of the effects of an inquiry-based science unit on students' problem-solving skills. The researcher tests the students three times in the month following the unit to examine the duration of the effects.

Replicate: To repeat a research study using the same method and similar participants. A successful replication obtains the same results as the original study.

Representative sample: A subset of a population used in a research study whose characteristics are generally reflective of the characteristics of the larger population that the sample is taken to represent. If a sample is not representative of the larger population, then any conclusions based on the sample might not hold for the larger population.

> *Example:* To find out whether senior boys in a high school have different academic interests than senior girls, a researcher interviews 10 percent of the senior boys and girls. If this 10 percent does not have roughly the same proportion of white and minority students as the entire class, however, any conclusions the researcher draws from the sample might not reflect the interests of all of the senior boys and girls.

Research design: The plan for how data will be collected in a research study. The research design should be appropriate for the research question that the study addresses. Research designs include simple descriptive, comparative descriptive, correlational, experimental, and quasi-experimental.

Research ethics: The system of moral values established for the conduct of research and codified by professional associations and the U.S. federal government.

Research method: In a research report, the details on how a research study was conducted, including the research design, the data-collection instruments, and the procedure.

Research problem: The purpose of the research study, usually described in more general terms than research questions.

> *Example:* A researcher conducts a study of a new standards-based mathematics curriculum to determine whether the curriculum benefits students at different grade levels differently. The research problem is whether the new mathematics curriculum has different effects at different grade levels.

Research question: The question that a research study is designed to answer. Research questions include: What is happening? How is it happening? Why is it happening? Is something causing an effect?

Research synthesis: A comprehensive and systematic summary and review of past empirical research or evaluation studies on a specific topic. (Another term for a research synthesis is literature review.) Research syntheses can be quantitative or qualitative. Meta-analysis is the term used for a quantitative synthesis, and narrative review is the term used for a qualitative synthesis.

Researcher bias: Errors in the results of a research or evaluation study due to influences from the researcher's or evaluator's expectancies concerning study outcomes.

> *Example:* A curriculum developer designs a new mathematics program for middle school students. If the developer conducts research on the effectiveness of the curriculum, the developer's expectancies could produce a positive bias in the results. To avoid researcher bias, persons and agencies that are external and independent from program developers should conduct the research.

Response rate: The proportion of participants in a study who respond to a data-collection instrument; typically refers to the number of persons who complete and return a mailed (or e-mailed) questionnaire.

Rival explanation: An alternate explanation for research results that rivals the researcher's conclusions.

> *Example:* A researcher randomly assigns eight elementary schools to participate in reform model A and eight elementary schools to participate in reform model B. The researcher measures student achievement prior to implementation of the reform models (the pretest). After one school year, the researcher measures student achievement again (the posttest). Because the students in the schools that used reform model B experienced achievement gains that were significantly higher than the students in schools that used reform model A, the researcher concludes that model B caused greater achievement gains. The main rival explanation is that events that occurred between the pretest and posttest could have influenced the results. For example, perhaps a large number of teachers in model B schools enrolled in graduate school, which improved their teaching. The researcher should demonstrate that historical events did not influence the results for either of the comparison groups.

Sample: A subset of individuals or entities from a population.

> *Example:* For the population of all fourth grade students in Kansas, the fourth grade students in the eastern half of the state would constitute a sample of the population (but not a random or a representative sample).

Sample attrition: A threat to the validity of research conclusions due to the loss of participants from a study sample (also referred to as mortality).

> *Example:* A researcher conducts a study of an after-school reading program on achievement gains. Twenty percent of the children drop out of the program. Conclusions about the effectiveness of the program are threatened by sample attrition because the students who remained could have special characteristics—for example, more motivation than those who left. Program effectiveness could be due to these individual characteristics and not the program characteristics.

Sample size: The number of participants (for example, students) or entities (for example, schools) in a study sample. Large samples are preferred because, if randomly selected, they are more representative of the population than small samples.

Scaled questionnaire: A data-collection instrument that gathers information about participants' attitudes or beliefs concerning a particular topic based on the degree of intensity that they indicate in their responses. (Also called an attitude scale.)

> *Example:* A scaled questionnaire on high school students' attitudes toward school might include a response scale and items such as the following:

Response Scale: Strongly Disagree, Disagree, Agree, Strongly Agree

   1. Teachers at my school are happy that I am in their classes.
   2. I look forward to attending school each day.

Scientifically-based research: According to the No Child Left Behind Act, research that is rigorous, systematic, objective, empirical, peer reviewed, and relies on multiple measurements and observations, preferably through experimental or quasi-experimental methods. According to the National Research Council (2002), six principles underlie all scientific research:

1. Pose significant questions that can be investigated empirically
2. Link research to relevant theory

3. Use methods that permit direct investigation of the question

4. Provide a coherent and explicit chain of reasoning

5. Replicate and generalize across studies

6. Disclose research to encourage professional scrutiny and critique

Secondary source: A description or summary of one or more prior research studies.

Selection bias: Systematic effects on the dependent variable that occur due to characteristics of the study participants.

> *Example:* A researcher conducts a study on the influence of student teaching on teaching performance. The researcher assigns twenty teacher-preparation candidates who attend college during the day to participate in sixteen weeks of student teaching. The researcher assigns twenty candidates who are night students to eight weeks of student teaching. Selection bias in this study is likely because the characteristics of day and night students, such as age and motivation, might be different. The results could be due to these differences instead of the amount of student teaching.

Simple descriptive research design: A research design in which data are collected to describe persons, organizations, settings, or phenomena.

> *Example:* A researcher surveys administrators of ten alternative teacher-preparation programs in order to describe the characteristics of the different programs.

Standard deviation: A measure of the variability of the scores in a set of scores or a frequency distribution, equivalent to the average distance of the scores from the mean.

> *Example:* The mean for the following set of five scores is 11 and the standard deviation is 2: 9, 10, 10, 12, 14. The scores vary on average about two points from the mean. For the following set of five scores, the mean is 10 and the standard deviation is 0: 10, 10, 10, 10, 10. There is no variation among the scores.

Standard error of estimate: In a graph of the relationship between two variables, a measure equivalent to the average distance between the actual data points and the regression line.

Standard score: A score that transforms an original or raw score into standard deviation units in order to locate the score's position within a frequency distribution. Standard scores also are known as z-scores and are calculated as: $z = $ (Raw Score − Mean)/Standard Deviation. The sign of a standard score (plus or minus) indicates whether it is above or below the mean.

Example: For the following set of five scores, the mean is 11 and the standard deviation is 2: 9, 10, 10, 12, 14. The score of 12 has a standard score of +0.50. The score of 9 has a standard score of –1.00.

Figure B.6 shows the raw scores transformed to standard scores.

Standardized test: A test that has standard items and standard procedures for administration and scoring. Standardized tests are prepared by commercial-test developers who establish the validity and reliability of the tests.

Example: The tests that are administered as part of the National Assessment of Educational Progress (NAEP) are standardized tests (see http://nces.ed.gov/nationsreportcard/).

Statistical control: The use of statistics to isolate the effects of an extraneous variable on the dependent variable in a research study.

Example: A researcher conducts a correlational study of the relationship of student achievement in mathematics to the amount of time spent on whole-class instruction. To statistically control for the influence of students' prior achievement, the researcher uses a multiple regression analysis in which the predictor variables are prior achievement and instructional time, making it possible to estimate the separate effects of each variable on student mathematics achievement, the dependent variable.

FIGURE B.6

Standard Scores

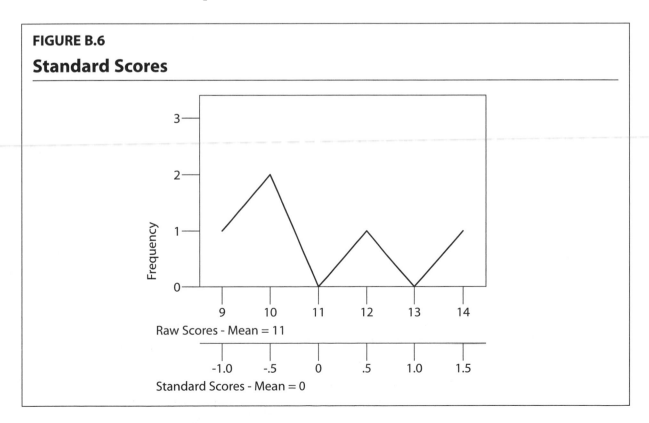

Statistical power: The likelihood that an inferential statistical test (for example, *t*-test, analysis of variance) will detect a statistically significant result when an actual treatment effect exists. The power of a statistical test increases as the sample size increases.

Statistically significant: A result that has a low probability (usually 5 percent) of occurring by chance. Because it is unlikely that a statistically significant result has occurred by chance, the result is said to reflect nonchance factors in the study, such as the effects of a treatment.

Statistics: Methods and rules for organizing and interpreting quantitative observations.

Stratified random sample: A sample of research participants that is randomly selected from different groups or strata in the population. The groups are defined based on one or more characteristics that might influence research results.

> *Example:* In a study of the influence of state standards on mathematics achievement, a researcher divides the state's population of middle school students into males and females. The researcher randomly selects participants for the study from within each group. The proportion of male and female participants selected for the sample reflects the proportion of males and females in the middle school student population.

Structural equation modeling (SEM): A statistical technique that tests a hypothesized network of linear relationships between observed and unobserved variables (also called latent variables).

> *Example:* A researcher hypothesizes that teachers' years of experience and their perceptions of school culture influence how much they learn from staff development, which in turn influences student achievement. (See Figure B.7.) Teacher experience, perceptions of school culture, and student achievement are observed variables, and teacher learning from staff development is an unobserved or latent variable. The researcher uses SEM to test whether the hypothesized model is supported by the data that the researcher collects on the observed variables.

Subjects: The participants whose behavior is examined in a research study.

Survey: A data-collection method in which participants provide information through self-report on questionnaires or in interviews.

FIGURE B.7

Structural Equation Modeling

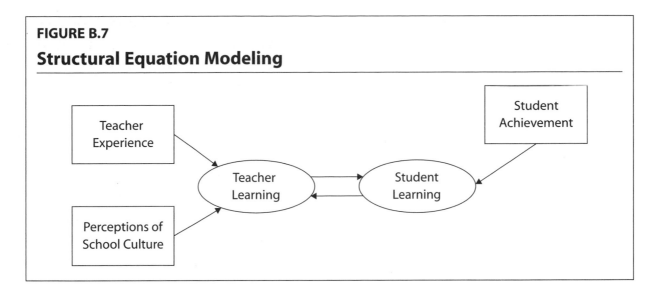

Test: A data-collection instrument that gathers information about participants' knowledge and skills related to a particular topic based on their responses to a standard set of questions.

Theory: A set of interrelated principles proposed as an explanation for phenomena or observations (also referred to as a conceptual framework).

> *Example:* Freud's theory of personality and Piaget's theory of child development are examples of social science theories. An example of a conceptual framework is an explanation of teacher professional development—in which teacher learning influences instruction, which in turn influences student achievement.

Threats to validity: Specific factors in a research study that threaten the validity or accuracy of research conclusions. (Also referred to as rival explanations.)

> *Example:* The loss of participants from the treatment or control group is a threat to validity because those who remain in the study could be different from those who left. Also, if more participants leave one group than the other, the two groups are no longer equivalent in nontreatment characteristics.

Treatment: The program, policy, or practice that is being studied through research or evaluation. Treatments are often interventions of some type such as a special reading program for low-achieving students. In an experimental research study, the treatment is the independent variable.

Treatment diffusion: The adoption of elements of the treatment in a research study by the participants who are in a control or a comparison group. Treatment diffusion (also called treatment spillover) threatens the validity of a conclusion that a treatment has no effect because both groups of participants experience the treatment.

> *Example:* A researcher randomly assigns teachers in an elementary school either to participate in weekly professional development on integrating technology with instruction (the treatment group) or to have an extra weekly planning time (the control group). Treatment diffusion is likely because treatment teachers can discuss the new techniques they are learning with control teachers, who then might adopt these techniques.

Treatment fidelity: The degree to which the treatment (that is, a program or intervention) in a research or evaluation study is implemented as planned or intended.

Treatment group: The group of participants in an experiment who receive some amount of the independent variable (that is, the program, policy, or practice being studied).

Triangulation: Comparison of results obtained from the use of multiple research methods or data-collection strategies in a single study.

> *Example:* A researcher randomly assigns half of the students in an after-school program to receive tutoring in reading and the other half to participate in a physical education class. The researcher examines students' gains in reading achievement and also interviews the students in each group about the effects of the after-school activity. The interview data are triangulated with the achievement data to confirm the information about the effects of the after-school program on achievement.

T-test: A statistical technique used to make inferences about a population of study participants based on a sample of these participants, or to test for statistically significant differences between two groups of observations.

Validity (of a measuring instrument): The degree to which an instrument measures what it is designed to measure and the degree to which it is used appropriately.

> *Example:* A valid test of mathematics should measure mathematics knowledge or skills and should be correlated with other measures of mathematics ability. A valid use of this test is to make inferences about knowledge of mathematics. For example, using the test to make inferences about reading skills would be invalid.

Validity (of a research study): The degree to which the conclusions of a research study are supported by evidence and can be trusted (also referred to as internal validity).

Variability: The amount of differences among scores in a distribution (that is, a set of scores); the degree to which the scores are spread out or are clustered together. When all of the scores in a distribution are the same, there is no variability among the scores. (See Figure B.8 for an example.)

FIGURE B.8

Variability

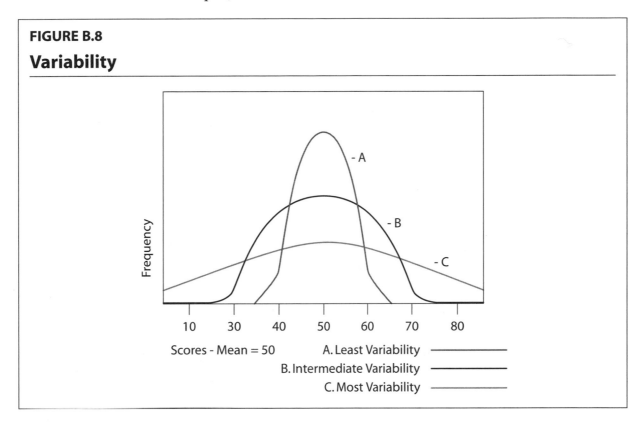

Variable: A characteristic or quantity that can change and have different values.

> *Example:* Variables studied in education include characteristics of students (for example, achievement), teachers (for example, certification), schools (curriculum), districts (leadership), teacher preparation programs (accreditation), and states (education funding).

Verification methods: Methods used in qualitative research to confirm the validity and reliability of the data coding and analyses.

Appendix C

Finding Education Research

The Educational Resources Clearing Center (ERIC)

ERIC is a federally funded national system that provides access to education-related literature. ERIC provides a wealth of information for researchers, practitioners, and policymakers. To appreciate fully what ERIC has to offer, spend some time exploring the ERIC Website at http://www.eric.ed.gov.

Before actually beginning an ERIC search, it is important to understand that every journal article and document entered into the ERIC database is assigned several ERIC "descriptors," which are terms with standard definitions. The trick is to determine which ERIC descriptors have been assigned to a particular topic or set of documents of interest. Fortunately, there is an ERIC Thesaurus that operates much like a standard thesaurus. By looking up terms in the ERIC Thesaurus related to a topic, it is possible to identify the ERIC descriptors used to index ERIC citations. These descriptors can then be used to conduct a search for the citations in the ERIC database. Tips for searching ERIC are provided on the ERIC Website.

Other Online Databases

Although ERIC is probably the largest online database of education research, there are other online databases that are resources for finding education-related research. Libraries of institutions of higher education usually subscribe to these databases, and members of the institution have access to them. Often members of the general public with proper identification can use the libraries of their state-supported institutions of higher education.

Other databases that have citations for education research include the following:

PsychInfo—Citations for the research in psychology and related areas such as education

Dissertation Abstracts—Abstracts of dissertations completed in the United States and in some foreign countries

Education Index—Citations of education-related articles from over six hundred sources, with access to full-text articles at some libraries

Searching the World Wide Web

Many articles on education research exist as online documents on the World Wide Web. Success in searching for such documents depends on Internet searching skills. Help with Internet searching techniques is available at the following Web site: http://library.albany.edu/internet.

Caution: The requirements for posting articles on Websites of organizations vary greatly. Some articles undergo a **peer review** that is similar to the review required for articles submitted to journals for publication. Other articles, however, are posted because the research supports the organization's views. Always evaluate the quality of the research that is reported in online articles.

Electronic Journals

Some education research journals exist online, such as *Education Policy Analysis Archives*, available at http://epaa.asu.edu/epaa/. With an electronic journal, it is possible to download and print full-text articles on education research.

U.S. Department of Education Website

An important online source for education research is the Website of the U.S. Department of Education (ED). Search for education research at http://www.ed.gov/index.jhtml, which provides access to more than 200 ED-sponsored Websites and more than 150 other federal agencies. An ED search can result in thousands of citations; for help with searching techniques, go to http://www.ed.gov/search/tips/index.html.

For access to a wide range of education statistics, see the Website of the National Center for Education Statistics (NCES) at http://nces.ed.gov/index.html. NCES produces hundreds of reports based on its many data-collection efforts, including reports on the National Assessment of Educational Progress (NAEP) and on the Schools and Staffing Survey (SASS).

What Works Clearinghouse

The U.S. Department of Education's Institute of Education Sciences established the What Works Clearinghouse (WWC) in 2002 to provide an independent source of evidence on what works in education. The WWC intends to provide policymakers and educators the information needed to make decisions about education programs and interventions based on high-quality, scientifically-based research. Consult the WWC Website for more details: http://www.whatworks.ed.gov/.

Manual Searches

It is possible to conduct manual searches for education research by using the print versions of indexes for journals and abstracts. These indexes are available at most higher education libraries. Two examples of relevant indexes are the *Current Index to Journals in Education*, published by ERIC, and *Psychological Abstracts*, published by the American Psychological Association. Some of the principles used for computer searches apply to manual searches. For example, it is important to determine the terms or descriptors used to identify articles related to a particular topic. Often a thesaurus that helps identify keywords to use in searches on different topics accompanies the index. With manual searches, it is generally a good idea to start with the most recent index because recent studies provide citations on prior research, which shortens the search process (McMillan, 2000).

Appendix D

Statistics Tutorial

Statistics refers to methods and rules for organizing and interpreting quantitative observations (Gravetter & Wallnau, 1988). The purpose of this tutorial is to explain basic statistical concepts commonly used in education research. The goal is to help readers understand the results reported in **quantitative education research.**

Descriptive Statistics

Descriptive statistics are used to describe sets of numbers such as test scores. Researchers organize sets of scores into tables and graphs called **frequency distributions.**

> Example 1: The following numbers represent students' scores on a reading test: 19, 23, 17, 27, 21, 20, 17, 22, 19, 17, 25, 21, 29, 24.

A frequency table (see Table D.1) shows the distribution or number of students who achieved a particular score on the reading test. In Example 1, three students achieved a score of 17.

A frequency graph (see Figure D.1) also shows the distribution or number of students who achieved a particular score.

TABLE D.1

Frequency Table

Reading Score	Frequency	Percent	Percentile
17	3	21.4	21.4
19	2	14.3	35.7
20	1	7.1	42.9
21	2	14.3	57.1
22	1	7.1	64.3
23	1	7.1	71.4
24	1	7.1	78.6
25	1	7.1	85.7
27	1	7.1	92.9
29	1	7.1	100.0
Totals	14	100.0	

FIGURE D.1

Frequency Graph

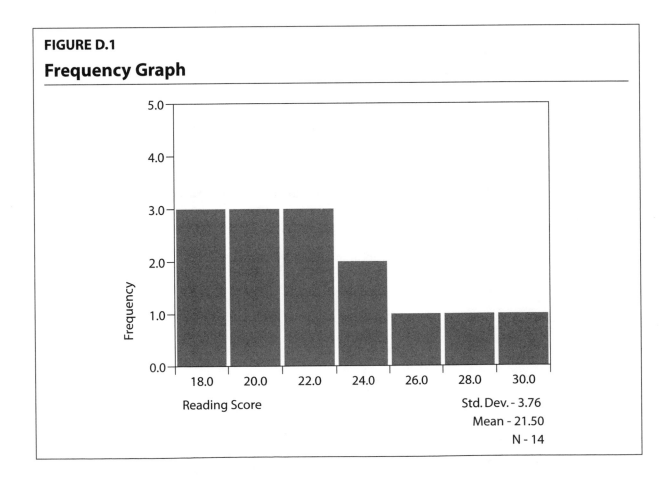

Std. Dev. - 3.76
Mean - 21.50
N - 14

The following are the most common statistics used to describe frequency distributions:

N: The number of scores in a *population*.

n: The number of scores in a *sample*.

Percent: The proportion of students in a frequency distribution who had a particular score. In Example 1, 21 percent of the students achieved a score of 17.

Percentile: The percentage of students in a frequency distribution who scored at or below a particular score (also referred to as percentile rank). In Example 1, 79 percent of the students achieved a score of 24 or lower, so a score of 24 is at the 79th percentile.

Mean: The average score in a frequency distribution. In Example 1, the mean score is 21.5. (Abbreviations for the mean are M if the scores are from a sample of participants and μ if the scores are from a population of participants.)

Median: The score in the middle of frequency distribution, or the score at the 50th percentile. In Example 1, the median score is 21.

Mode: The score that occurs most frequently in the distribution. In Example 1, the mode is 17.

Range: The difference between the highest and lowest score in the distribution. In Example 1, the range is 12.

Standard deviation: A measure of how much the scores vary from the mean. In Example 1, the standard deviation is 3.76, indicating that the average difference between the scores and mean is around four points. The higher the standard deviation, the more different the scores are from one another and from the mean. (Abbreviations for the standard deviation are SD if the scores are from a sample and σ if the scores are from a population.)

The mean, median, and mode are called measures of **central tendency** because they identify a single score as typical or representative of all the scores in a frequency distribution.

When a frequency distribution has a high standard deviation, the mean is not a good measure of central tendency, as in the following set of scores:

Example 2: Scores = 1, 4, 3, 4, 2, 7, 18, 3, 7, 2, 4, 3;
Mean = 5; Median = 3.5; Standard Deviation = 4.53.

The standard deviation in Example 2 indicates that the average difference between each score and the mean is around 4.5 points. Only one score (18), however, is 4.5 or more points different from the mean. In this example, the one extreme score (18) overly influences the mean. The median (3.5) is a better measure of central tendency because extreme scores do not influence the median.

> **Standard score:** Specifies the location of an original score or **raw score** within a frequency distribution, based on standard deviation units. Standard scores also are known as z-scores and are calculated as follows: z = (Raw Score – Mean)/Standard Deviation.

In Example 1, a raw score of 27 has a standard score of +1.46 [(27 – 21.5)/3.76]. This indicates that a score of 27 is 1.46 standard deviation units above the mean. A raw score of 19 has a standard score of –0.66, indicating that it is 0.66 standard deviation units below the mean.

Standard scores make it possible to compare scores on different tests that have different means and standard deviations. For example, Table D.2 shows a student's raw scores and standard scores on different tests.

On which test did this student perform best in comparison to the rest of the students in the class? Numerically, the student's highest score was on the language arts test, but the standard score for language arts indicates that the student performed worst on this test because the score was 1.1 standard deviation units below the mean. The student's best performance was on the mathematics test in which the student scored 0.75 standard deviation units above the mean. Note that although the student had the same score of 42 on the science and social studies tests, the score was above the mean in social studies but below the mean in science. The frequency curve in Figure D.2 illustrates these comparisons.

TABLE D.2

Standard Scores

Subject	Raw Score	Standard Score
Mathematics	31	+.75
Language Arts	71	–1.10
Science	42	–.25
Social Studies	42	+.56

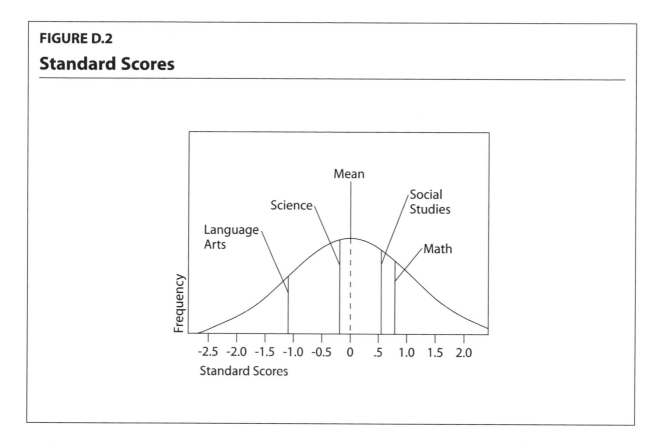

FIGURE D.2
Standard Scores

Inferential Statistics

Researchers use **inferential statistics** to make inferences about a population of study participants based on a sample of these participants. For example, a researcher might attempt to conclude something about a population of students (for instance, all fourth graders in a school district) by studying a sample of these students. Based on inferential statistics, the researcher infers that the results from the sample of fourth graders are also true of the population of fourth graders. Inferential statistics also are used to make inferences about the differences between two or more groups of observations.

> Example 3: A researcher randomly selects participants from a population of fourth grade students and randomly assigns them to two groups. Students in Group A participate in Reading Program A. Students in Group B participate in Reading Program B. Based on their reading test scores, which program resulted in better reading performance? (See Table D.3, Table D.4, and Figure D.3.)

TABLE D.3

Programs A and B Reading Scores

Program A Scores	Program B Scores
14	15
11	22
15	19
15	20
16	22
16	20
18	21
18	14
17	20
18	21
14	19
17	19
12	16
15	12
16	18
14	17
15	20
13	18
$n = 18$	$n = 18$
$M = 15.22$	$M = 18.5$
$SD = 2.02$	$SD = 2.77$

TABLE D.4

Programs A and B

Reading Score	Frequency	Percent	Percentile
Program A			
11	1	5.6	5.6
12	1	5.6	11.1
13	1	5.6	16.7
14	3	16.7	33.3
15	4	22.2	55.6
16	3	16.7	72.2
17	2	11.1	83.3
18	3	16.7	100.0
Program B			
12	1	5.6	5.6
14	1	5.6	11.1
15	1	5.6	16.7
16	1	5.6	22.2
17	1	5.6	27.8
18	2	11.1	38.9
19	3	16.7	55.6
20	4	22.2	77.8
21	2	11.1	89.9
22	2	11.1	100.0

FIGURE D.3

Frequency Graph for Programs A and B

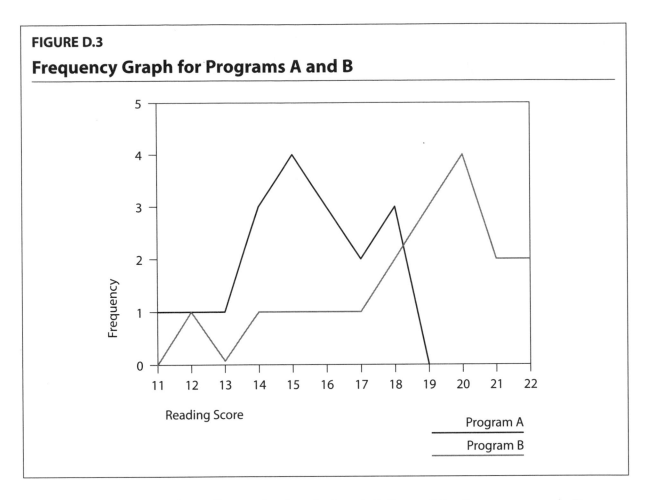

According to the descriptive statistics and the frequency graph, Program B resulted in better reading performance because students in Group B achieved a higher mean test score than students in Group A. Is this difference, however, of 3.28 between the means of the two groups due to Program B, or could this difference simply be due to chance factors? To answer this question requires the use of inferential statistics.

Statistical Significance

The research design of the study determines the type of inferential statistic used. All inferential statistics, however, answer the same question: Could these findings occur by chance or are these findings too unlikely to occur by chance and therefore the findings reflect a real effect of what is being studied?

The most common inferential statistics are the *t*-test and the **analysis of variance**. The *t* statistic is used when there are two groups of participants in the research study. The *F* statistic is used when there are more than two groups in the research study. Usually, the researcher uses a computer program to calculate the inferential test statistic and the probability of obtaining a particular statistical value if there is no real difference between the groups.

In Example 3, the t statistic is 4.06. The researcher would report this result as follows: Students in Group B performed significantly better than students in Group A, $t = 4.06$ (34) $p < 0.001$. What does this mean?

Simply put, the probability of this result occurring by chance is less than one time out of 1,000. Therefore, the researcher can be very confident that the difference between the two groups reflects an actual difference. [*Note:* The number 34 in parentheses is called the **degrees of freedom** and reflects the size of the samples. For a two-sample t-test, the degrees of freedom are calculated as $(n - 1) + (n - 1)$. Degrees of freedom are used in the calculation of inferential statistics, and it is conventional to report them.]

The term **statistically significant** is used to describe results for which there is a 5 percent or less probability that the results occurred by chance. Why 5 percent? By convention, social scientists have chosen this percentage as the cut-off point (although other percentages are sometimes chosen). Therefore, any result that has a probability of occurring by chance more than five times out of 100 (designated by convention as $p > 0.05$) is reported as not significant. Researchers should not discuss nonsignificant results as though they indicate actual differences between groups.

Sometimes researchers also report the **confidence interval** for the results of a t-test. In Example 2, the 95 percent confidence interval for the mean difference between Programs A and B is between 1.63 and 4.92. This means that if the entire population of fourth grade students participated in the two reading programs, there is a 95 percent probability that the mean difference in reading achievement between Programs A and B would be between 1.63 and 4.92 points. The confidence interval provides an estimate of population measurements based on sample measurements.

There is an important relationship between the size of the sample and statistical significance. As the sample size increases, the probability increases that significant differences will be detected. This is a concept called **statistical power.**

Consider results from the following studies:

> Example 4: Program X: $n = 10$, Mean achievement $= 30.5$; Program Y: $n = 10$, Mean achievement $= 31.5$; $t = 2.15$, $p > .05$. The difference between Program X and Program Y is not statistically significant.

> Example 5: Program X: $n = 100$, Mean achievement $= 30.5$; Program Y: $n = 100$, Mean achievement $= 31.5$; $t = 2.15$, $p < 0.05$. The difference between Program X and Program Y is statistically significant.

The same numerical difference of 1.5 points between the two groups is statistically significant in the study with large sample sizes (and more statistical power) but not in the study with small sample sizes. In studies with very large sample sizes (for example, 1,000), even small numerical differences can be statistically significant. For this reason, it is important to examine what is known as the **effect size** of a statistically significant difference.

Practical Significance

In addition to measures of statistical significance, researchers frequently calculate and report measures of **practical significance,** known as the **effect size.** The effect size helps educators and policymakers decide whether a statistically significant difference between programs translates into enough of a difference to justify adoption of a program.

There are different ways to measure effect sizes. One commonly used measure is called Cohen's d, which measures effect sizes in standard deviation units. In Example 3, Cohen's $d = 1.34$ standard deviation units. Social scientists commonly interpret d as follows (although interpretation also depends on the **intervention** and the **dependent variable**):

- Small effect sizes: $d = .2$ to $.5$

- Medium effect sizes: $d = .5$ to $.8$

- Large effect sizes: $d = .8$ and higher

Thus, in Example 3, the effect size of $d = 1.34$ is "large," but what does "large" mean in terms of reading achievement?

A simple way to understand effect sizes is to translate d into percentile gains. An effect size of $d = 1.34$ translates into a percentile gain of 41 percentile points (based on the **normal curve,** as described in the next section). This means that the reading score of the average student who participates in Reading Program B will be 41 percentile points higher than the average student who participates in Reading Program A. The bottom line: Program B is a more effective reading program than Program A.

The Normal Curve and Effect Sizes

Another way to understand effect sizes is to examine the normal curve. The normal curve refers to a frequency distribution in which the graph of scores resembles a bell—hence, the famous bell-shaped curve. Many human traits such as intelligence, personality scores, and student achievement have **normal distributions.**

> Example 6: If all adults in the state of Colorado were given a general intelligence test, the frequency distribution of the scores would resemble the bell-shaped curve shown in Figure D.4.

FIGURE D.4

Frequency Graph of Intelligence

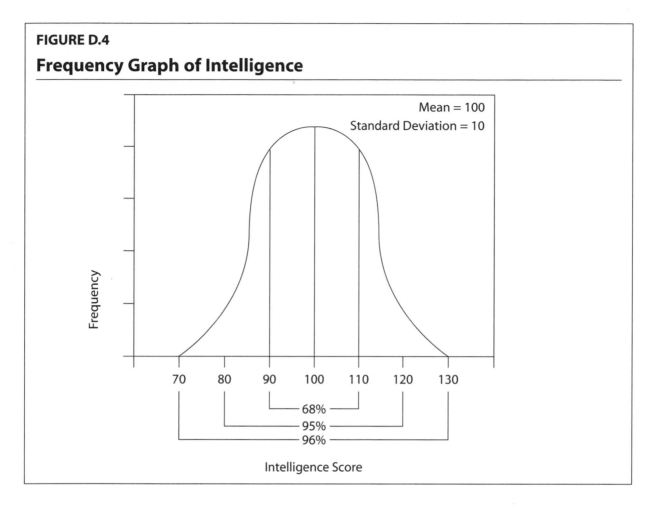

The normal distribution has an important characteristic. The mean, median, and mode are the same score (a score of 100 in Example 6) because a normal distribution is symmetrical. The score with the highest frequency occurs in the middle of the distribution and exactly half of the scores occur above the middle and half of the scores occur below. Most of the scores occur around the middle of the distribution or the mean. Very high and very low scores occur infrequently and are therefore considered rare.

In a normal distribution, 34.1 percent of the scores occur between the mean and one standard deviation above the mean. In Example 6, the standard deviation is 10. The result is that 34.1 percent of adults in Colorado scored between 100 and 110. (Conversely, 34.1 percent of adults in Colorado scored between 100 and 90.) A score of 120 is two standard deviations above the mean. In a normal distribution, 47.5 percent of the scores occur between the mean and two standard deviations above or below the mean. Thus, two standard deviations above and below the mean include 95 percent of all scores.

Scores in a normal distribution also can be described as percentiles. The score that is the mean (and also the median and mode) is the score at the 50th percentile because 50 percent of the scores are at that score or below.

In the example, a score of 100 is at the 50th percentile. A score of 110 is one standard deviation above the mean and therefore at the 84th percentile (50 percent + 34.1 percent). Finally, a score of 120 is two standard deviations above the mean and is therefore at the 97th percentile (50 percentile + 47.5 percentile).

Hint: Sometimes percentile scores on tests are converted into **normal curve equivalent (NCE) scores** because NCE scores are easier to manipulate arithmetically and statistically than are percentiles.

How do effect sizes relate to the normal curve? Because Cohen's d is measured in standard deviation units, an effect size of $d = 1.0$ is equal to one standard deviation above the mean.

> Example 7: A researcher discovers a special herb that increases adult intelligence, with an effect size of $d = 1.0$. (See Figure D.5.) The average adult in Colorado (with an intelligence score of 100) who takes this herb can expect to have an intelligence score of 110, an increase in percentile rank from the 50th percentile to the 84th percentile. This researcher stands to make a lot of money!

FIGURE D.5

Effect Size

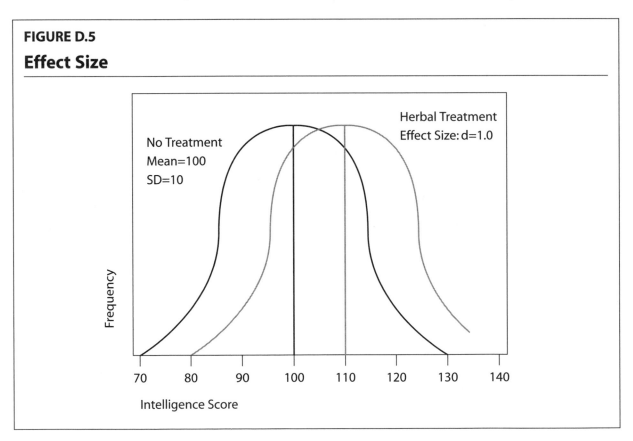

Effect sizes also apply to scores on student achievement tests because these tests are designed to be normally distributed. For example, an effect size of $d = 1.0$ for a reading program means that the reading program increased the reading score of the average student to one standard deviation above the mean. An effect size of $d = 0.5$ means that the reading score of the average student in the program increased to 0.5 standard deviation above the mean. (If the standard deviation equals 8, the average student's score would increase by 8 points with $d = 1.0$, and would increase by 4 points with $d = 0.5$.)

Caution: Effect sizes also can be negative, which means that scores are lowered by the effect of the program in the study. For example, an effect size of $d = -1.0$ means that the average score was decreased by one standard deviation.

Correlation

Correlation refers to a technique used to measure the relationship between two or more **variables.**

> Example 8: In Table D.5, the first variable is the number of students in fourth grade classes in a school district. The second variable is the mean reading score of each class.

TABLE D.5

Example 8

Variable 1 Class Size	Variable 2 Mean Reading Score
25	70
20	80
25	60
25	72
30	58
22	71
28	68
20	75
19	72
29	61

Pearson *r* is a statistic that is commonly used to calculate **bivariate correlations.** In Example 8, Pearson $r = -.80$, $p < .01$. What does this mean?

To interpret correlations, four pieces of information are necessary (Gravetter & Wallnau, 1988).

1. *The numerical value of the correlation coefficient.* **Correlation coefficients** can vary numerically between 0.0 and 1.0. The closer the correlation is to 1.0, the stronger the relationship between the two variables. A correlation of 0.0 indicates the absence of a relationship. In Example 8, the correlation coefficient is –0.80, which indicates the presence of a strong relationship.

2. *The sign of the correlation coefficient.* A positive correlation coefficient means that as variable 1 increases, variable 2 increases, and conversely, as variable 1 decreases, variable 2 decreases. In other words, the variables move in the same direction when there is a positive correlation. A negative correlation means that as variable 1 increases, variable 2 decreases and vice versa. In other words, the variables move in opposite directions when there is a negative correlation. In Example 8, the negative sign indicates that as class size increases, mean reading scores decrease.

3. *The statistical significance of the correlation.* A statistically significant correlation is indicated by a probability value of less than 0.05. This means that the probability of obtaining such a correlation coefficient by chance is less than five times out of 100, so the result indicates the presence of a relationship. In Example 8, there is a statistically significant negative relationship between class size and reading score ($p < .001$), such that the probability of this correlation occurring by chance is less than one time out of 1,000.

4. *The effect size of the correlation.* For correlations, the effect size is called the **coefficient of determination** and is defined as r^2. The coefficient of determination can vary from 0 to 1.00 and indicates the proportion of variation in the scores that can be predicted from the relationship between the two variables. In Example 8, the coefficient of determination is 0.65, which means that 65 percent of the variation in mean reading scores among the different classes can be explained from the relationship between class size and reading scores. (Conversely, 35 percent of the variation in mean reading scores cannot be explained.)

A correlation can only indicate the presence or absence of a relationship, not the nature of the relationship. In Example 8, it cannot be concluded that smaller class sizes cause higher reading scores, even if the correlation is 1.0. *Correlation is not causation.* There is always the possibility that a third variable influenced the results. For example, perhaps the students in the small classes were higher in verbal ability than the students in the large classes or were from higher-income families or had higher-quality teachers.

Correlation and Prediction

Another use of correlation is prediction. A mathematical technique called **regression analysis** uses the correlation between two variables to predict the values for variable 2 (the dependent or **criterion variable**) based on the values for variable 1 (the **predictor variable**).

Figure D.6 indicates a linear relationship between variable 1 and variable 2 from Example 8.

FIGURE D.6

Graph of a Linear Relationship

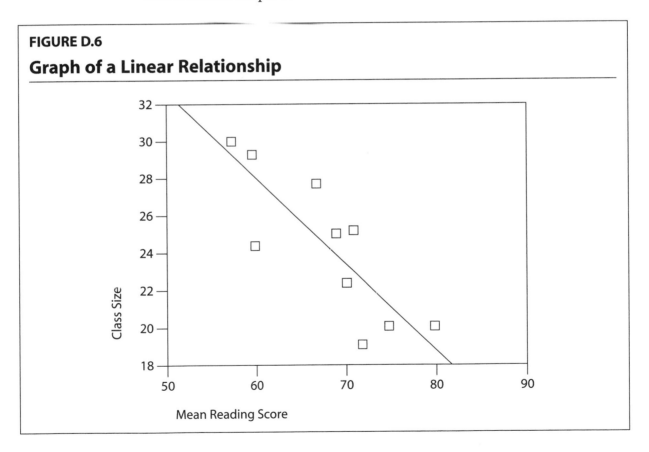

A regression analysis can identify the equation that best describes the linear relationship between class size and reading score in the graph. This equation can then be used to estimate mean reading scores based on class sizes. Unless there is a perfect correlation between two variables (that is, $r = \pm 1.00$), the prediction based on regression analysis will be imperfect. The **standard error of estimate** indicates how accurately the equation can predict values of a variable. In the example, the standard error of estimate is 4.44, which is the average distance between the regression line equation and the actual data points for the mean reading scores. (See Figure D.7.)

A simple way to think about prediction error is that the smaller the numerical value of the correlation, the smaller the coefficient of determination, and the more error there will be when using the correlation for prediction.

FIGURE D.7

Graph 2

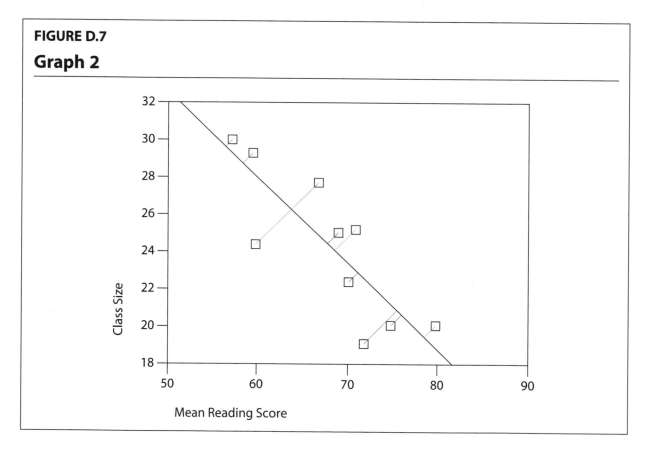

Correlation with Multiple Variables

When there is more than one predictor variable, the technique of **multiple regression analysis** combines the predictor variables to produce a multiple correlation coefficient called R (Grimm & Yarnold, 1995). For example, in addition to class size, a researcher might use students' mean verbal ability scores and socioeconomic status to predict reading scores. A multiple correlation coefficient of $R = 0.71$ would indicate the degree of the combined correlation of the predictor variables with mean reading scores. The squared multiple correlation coefficient of $R^2 = 0.49$ would indicate that 49 percent of the variation among mean reading scores of the different fourth grade classes can be explained by the relationship between reading scores and the combination of class size, verbal ability, and socioeconomic status. (Conversely, 51 percent of the variation in mean reading scores cannot be explained.)

Although the technique of multiple regression provides more information than bivariate correlation, it cannot be concluded that variables caused other variables to occur in certain ways.

Structural Equation Modeling

Like multiple regression, **structural equation modeling** (SEM) also examines linear relationships among a set of variables (Maruyama, 1998). With SEM, however, the researcher hypothesizes a model for how the variables that are measured in a study are related to one another, as well as how the measured variables influence and are influenced by unobserved variables called **latent variables.** For example, student motivation might be a latent variable that influences student achievement, and class size might influence student motivation. (See Figure D.8.) In SEM, the statistics that are of primary interest are **goodness-of-fit statistics** that evaluate how well the data fit the researcher's proposed model for the interrelationships among the variables.

FIGURE D.8

Structural Equation Model

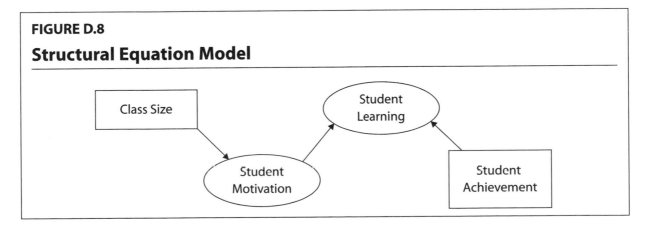

Caution: Structural equation modeling is sometimes referred to as causal path modeling. Despite the use of the word "causal," this technique is correlational and does not support conclusions about cause and effect.

Hierarchical Linear Modeling

Hierarchical linear modeling (HLM) is a statistical technique used when the data are from participants who exist within different levels of a hierarchical structure (Osborne, 2000). For example, students exist within a hierarchical structure that includes family, classroom, grade, school, district, and state. Student achievement is considered nested data because it reflects influences from each of these levels (for example, influences from family characteristics; the classroom teacher; the grade level; and school, district, and state policies).

With HLM, the researcher first measures the influence of one or more predictor variables (for example, student socioeconomic status and prior achievement) on an outcome (student reading achievement) at level one. Next the researcher measures the relationship of level two predictor variables (for example, teacher professional development and experience) on the level one relationship. Through HLM, a researcher might find that student socioeconomic status and prior achievement are negatively related to reading achievement, but that this relationship is less strong with increasing teacher professional development. In other words, the more professional development teachers have, the weaker the correlation of these other factors is with their students' achievement.

References

Allen, I. E., & Seaman, J. (2004). *Entering the mainstream: The quality and extent of online education in the United States, 2003 and 2004.* Needham, MA: Sloan Center for Online Education. Retrieved November 7, 2005, from http://www.sloan-c.org/resources/entering_mainstream.pdf.

Anfara, V. A., Brown, K. M., & Mangione, T. L. (2002). Qualitative analysis on stage: Making the research process more public. *Educational Researcher, 31*(7), 28–38.

Bandura, A. (1997). *Self-efficacy: The exercise of control.* New York: W. H. Freeman.

Bergin, D. A., Hudson, L. M., Chryst, C. F., & Resetar, M. (1992). An afterschool intervention program for educationally disadvantaged young children. *Urban Review, 24*(3), 203–217.

Blachman, B. A., Schatschneider, C., Fletcher, J. M., Francis, D. J., Clonan, S. M., Shaywitz, B. A., & Shaywitz, S. E. (2004). Effects of intensive reading remediation for second and third graders and a 1-year follow-up. *Journal of Educational Psychology, 90*(3), 444–461.

Blenis, D. S. (2000). *The effects of mandatory, competitive science fairs on fifth grade students' attitudes toward science and interests in science.* ERIC Document Reproduction Service No. ED 443 718.

Borman, G. D., Hewes, G. M., Overman, L. T., & Brown, S. (2003). Comprehensive school reform and achievement: A meta-analysis. *Review of Educational Research, 73*(2), 125–230.

Calhoun, E. F. (1994). *How to use action research in the self-renewing school.* Alexandria, VA: Association for Supervision and Curriculum Development.

Cooper, H. (1998). *Synthesizing research: A guide for literature reviews* (3rd ed.). Thousand Oaks, CA: Sage.

Cooper, H., Charlton, K., Valentine, J. C., & Muhlenbruck, L. (2000). Making the most of summer school: A meta-analytic and narrative review. *Monographs of the Society for Research in Child Development*, Serial No. 260, 65(1).

Creswell, J. W. (2002). *Research design: Qualitative, quantitative, and mixed method approaches.* Thousand Oaks, CA: Sage.

Dillman, D. A. (2000). *Mail and internet surveys: The tailored design method.* Hoboken, New Jersey: Wiley.

Gibson, S., & Dembo, M. (1984). Teacher efficacy: A construct validation. *Journal of Educational Psychology*, 76(4), 569–582.

Goddard, R. D., Hoy, W. K., & Hoy, A. W. (2000). Collective teacher efficacy: Its meaning, measure, and impact on student achievement. *American Educational Research Journal, 37*(2), 479–507.

Goddard, R. D., Logerfo, L., & Hoy, W. K. (2004). High school accountability: The role of perceived collective efficacy. *Educational Policy, 18*(3), 403–425.

Gravetter, F. J., & Wallnau, L. B. (1988). *Statistics for the behavioral sciences* (2nd ed.). St. Paul: West Publishing.

Grimm, L. G., & Yarnold, P. R. (Eds.). (1995). *Reading and understanding multivariate statistics.* Washington, DC: American Psychological Association.

Grisham, D. L., Laguardia, A., & Brink, B. (2000). Partners in professionalism: Creating a quality field experience for preservice teachers. *Action in Teacher Education, 21*(4), 27–40.

Guba, E. G., & Lincoln, Y. S. (1989). *Fourth generation evaluation.* Thousand Oaks, CA: Sage.

Hirsch, E. (2004). *Listening to the experts: A report on the 2004 South Carolina teacher working conditions survey.* Chapel Hill, NC: The Southeast Center for Teaching Quality.

Lauer, P. A., Akiba, M., Wilkerson, S. B., Apthorp, H. A., Snow, D., & Martin-Glenn, M. (2003*). The effectiveness of out-of-school-time strategies in assisting low-achieving students in reading and mathematics: A research synthesis.* Aurora, CO: Mid-continent Research for Education and Learning.

Marchant, G. J., & Paulson, S. E. (2005). The relationship of high school graduation exams to graduation rates and SAT scores. *Education Policy Analysis Archives, 13*(6). Retrieved November 7, 2005, from http://epaa.asu.edu/epaa/v13n6/.

Maruyama, G. M. (1998). *Basics of structural equation modeling.* Thousand Oaks, CA: Sage.

Massell, D., Kirst, M., & Hoppe, M. (1997). *Persistence and change: Standards-based systemic reform in nine states.* Philadelphia: Consortium for Policy Research in Education.

McMillan, J. H. (2000). *Education research: Fundamentals for the consumer* (3rd ed.). New York: Addison Wesley Longman.

National Commission on Excellence in Education. (1983). *A nation at risk: The imperative for educational reform.* Washington, DC: Government Printing Office.

National Council of Teachers of Mathematics. (1989). *Curriculum and evaluation standards for school mathematics.* Reston, VA: Author.

National Education Goals Panel. (1991). *The National Education Goals Report: Building a nation of learners.* Washington, DC: Author.

National Research Council. (2002). *Scientific research in education.* Committee on Scientific Principles for Education Research. Shavelson, R. J., & Towne, L., (Eds.). Center for Education. Division of Behavioral and Social Sciences and Education. Washington, DC: National Academy Press.

Onwuegbuzie, A. J., & Daniel, L. G. (2003). Typology of analytical and interpretational errors in quantitative and qualitative educational research. *Current Issues in Education, 6*(2). Retrieved November 7, 2005, from http://cie.ed.asu.edu/volume6/number2/.

Osborne, J. W. (2000). Advantages of hierarchical linear modeling. *ERIC/AE Digest.* ERIC Document Reproduction Service No. ED447198.

Ravitch, D. (1995). *National standards in American education: A citizen's guide.* Washington, DC: Brookings Institution.

Riordan, J. E., & Noyce, P. E. (2001). The impact of two standards-based mathematics curricula on student achievement in Massachusetts. *Journal for Research in Mathematics Education, 32*(4), 368–398.

Shadish, W. R., Cook, T. D., & Campbell, D. T. (2002). *Experimental and quasi-experimental designs for causal inference.* Boston: Houghton Mifflin.

Shanahan, T. (2000). Research synthesis: Making sense of the accumulation of knowledge in reading. In M. L. Kamil, P. B. Mosenthal, P. D. Pearson, & R. Barr (Eds.), *Handbook of reading research, volume III* (pp. 209–226). Mahwah, NJ: Erlbaum.

Sikula, J., Buttery, T. J., & Guyton, E. (Eds.). (1996). *Handbook of research on teacher education.* New York: Simon & Schuster Macmillan.

U.S. Department of Education. (2002). *U.S. Department of Education Strategic Plan.* Washington, DC: Office of the Deputy Secretary, Planning and Performance Management Service.

Wayne, A. J., & Youngs, P. (2003). Teacher characteristics and student achievement gains: A review. *Review of Educational Research, 73*(1), 89–122.

Weiss, C. H. (1998). *Evaluation: Methods for studying programs and policies* (2nd ed.). Upper Saddle River, NJ: Prentice Hall.

Windschitl, M., & Sahl, K. (2002). Tracing teachers' use of technology in a laptop computer school: The interplay of teacher beliefs, social dynamics, and institutional culture. *American Educational Research Journal, 39*(1), 165–205.

About the Author

PATRICIA A. LAUER wrote *An Education Research Primer* while employed as a principal researcher at Mid-continent Research for Education and Learning (McREL) in Denver, Colorado. At McREL she was responsible for conducting, analyzing, and reporting on research and evaluation studies related to teacher quality and school improvement, and she has written numerous technical reports related to this work. Her work includes studies of award-winning teacher-preparation programs, university–school partnerships, teacher learning in high-performing high-needs schools, and online professional development for rural teachers. She led a team of researchers in writing case studies of collaborative action research partnerships with school districts, which resulted in a chapter for *Effective Educational Partnerships* (2002, Praeger). She was also the lead author of a research synthesis on the effectiveness of out-of-school-time strategies in assisting low-achieving students in reading and mathematics. She has given presentations on her work at research conferences and has conducted workshops and trainings for school districts and universities.

Lauer received her B.A. in psychology from the University of Nebraska at Omaha and her M.A. and Ph.D. in experimental psychology from the University of Colorado at Boulder. Prior to joining McREL, she taught psychology and research methods at the college level for several years.

Lauer is now the Evaluation Director at Rocky Mountain Center for Health Promotion and Education, 7525 W. 10th Avenue, Lakewood, CO 80124. Phone: 303-239-6976, ext. 105. Fax: 303-239-8428. Email: patl@rmc.org.

Index